Awakenings
A Life's Journey

Shane Sacha

Awakenings
Copyright © 2020 by Shane Sacha

All rights reserved. No part of this publication may be reproduced, distributed, or transmitted in any form or by any means, including photocopying, recording, or other electronic or mechanical methods, without the prior written permission of the author, except in the case of brief quotations embodied in critical reviews and certain other non-commercial uses permitted by copyright law.

Tellwell Talent
www.tellwell.ca

ISBN
978-0-2288-4343-6 (Hardcover)
978-0-2288-4342-9 (Paperback)
978-0-2288-4344-3 (eBook)

Slowly, slowly when walls come down, we will cry, we will sob. As will a child when, after years of being ignored, in darkness, abandoned, judged, finally feels some rays of sunshine, a sense of warmth, of hope.

- SHANE SACHA

To all that have suffered and grown, relentlessly seeking answers, "you are my inspiration."

TABLE OF CONTENTS

Introduction vii

Chapter 1   Silence - What We Avoid is What We Need! 1
Chapter 2   A Childhood Experience 4
Chapter 3   Roughest Seas 11
Chapter 4   Broken 22
Chapter 5   Reflecting - The Key to Change 40
Chapter 6   Finding Worth - Be True to You 46
Chapter 7   Ebb and Flow - Letting Go 50
Chapter 8   Embracing Change - Breaking the Mould 53
Chapter 9   Self Worth - Where to Draw the Line 58
Chapter 10   Focus on You - Become Your Own Priority 62
Chapter 11   Stop the Delusion - Tricks of the Mind 65
Chapter 12   Negativity - Breaking the Cycle 73
Chapter 13   Trust What You Know and Feel, Not Your
             Desire 80
Chapter 14   True Wisdom Over Intelligence 85
Chapter 15   Meditation 87

Food for Thought 90

INTRODUCTION

I WOULD LIKE TO thank all those within these pages that have challenged me. This was key to my drive, ambition and more. There was only one way forward and I could not have done this without you. Ultimately, we all must learn to be responsible for our own thoughts, feelings and actions. Their contribution has enabled me to set myself free. I wish them peace and happiness always. Thank you.

This book is based on true events and includes real insights and self-discoveries.

This life's journey is hard. I hope by sharing this journey, these experiences and insights, that you may find your own strength, insight, compassion and courage toward yourself and others. For there is no greater journey to be had.

You are not alone. We are all suffering or have suffered from the negative and at times very destructive impact of our thoughts and ideas. Our thoughts can potentially destroy us and everything around us. I hope that while reading this book, you realise that *you* have the strength and capacity to not only pull yourself out of this debilitating cycle, but to become self-empowered and free from the limiting confines of your thoughts.

My inspiration for this book started a number of years ago as I began to understand the *concepts of self-help*. At times when walls within me came down, I slowly became freer, more energised. I wanted to share these experiences and I enjoyed connecting with others and their experiences.

When I first began writing a self-help book, I wrote because I thought I had discovered the truth within. I knew the concepts of spirituality and I knew them well! I thought I had found a place of neutrality. What I didn't know at that time was that soon I was to be challenged with all I thought I had broken through. All I had written about and more. The next three and a half years were by far the most intense, destructive and painful years of my life.

Those few years enabled me to strip down everything that I held dear within, all that I associated with meaning and true worth. It was a massive wake up call and In the end I discovered a truth within which set me free. This truth is within all, and discoverable by all. The intensity of my suffering was the key to unlocking that door. In an analogy I've used many times; whilst cooking a cake in the oven, it's the *intensity* which enables it to rise to the *perfection* it's meant for, it is a crucial factor. Without the intensity I not only would have maintained my suffering but actually have become more accustomed to it. I needed the shock factor of having nowhere to run. What a blessing in disguise. I was forced to let go of what I held dear to see what remained.

This intense suffering is not a prerequisite. I like to think it's not absolutely necessary. What lead to suffering for me and many others is the refusal to see, trust or investigate the subtle yet undeniable hints or prodding we feel that something isn't quite right within, or around us. At first, we begin to blame others or our circumstances for these feelings, maybe our government or even our world. We start to control our environment and the people around us in an attempt to alleviate what our gut is telling us. If this feeling is not challenged or investigated, eventually this will lead to more suffering, not just for us but also those around us. We try more and more to irrationally control a greater range of our friends and environment. Leading up to this, our subtle feelings grow and intensify and become very loud, causing us to go to new heights to try and distract ourselves from the truth, avoiding that uneasy feeling creating *dis-ease* within. The wake-up call by this stage is not a subtle 'whisper in our ear' but an almighty shove or crashing down of some false illusion we've been hiding or believing. Some of us still refuse this great gift of life, exposing our deluded mind in an illusionary world, till the day we die. But those that are hungry enough, those that have burned long and deep enough in the hellish realm of their irrational and destructive thoughts. They will embark on a most amazing journey… the journey of true self-discovery!

We are constantly growing, maturing, developing and experiencing on many levels. We are always evolving. Our awareness is pushed to expand all the time. If we don't facilitate this, we suffer!

It's hard to accurately speak about our own levels of development and it's impossible to know exactly where we are at. We like to believe that we are the most evolved amongst our peers and family, but this comparison often involves judging others and, in the process, justifying our viewpoint. We have all had so many different experiences throughout our lives and have dealt with or embraced them in so many varied ways that it's almost impossible to assess our position compared to another. Holding onto an idea of a specific level of development can be a major distraction or hurdle and it's absolutely not necessary. We are not competing with anyone but ourselves. It's not about who is in front, it's about who is willing to go all the way to discover their heart and free themselves from their mental and emotional burdens. At times someone appearing to be less developed than us may have a major awakening.

It can be confusing as to how a seemingly broken or confused person (someone you may think is less advanced than you) can have a major awakening. But it is ultimately because the key ingredient to awakening (discovering true heart) is purely to *surrender*. Although accumulation of knowledge is important, holding on to it like you own it or because you think it gives you value or credibility is a trap. One will never awaken until one relinquishes *ownership* of concepts and ideas. This is a very hard thing to grasp, but I hope this understanding will deepen as you read on.

I'm going to separate people into two basic groups before one awakens to the *truth*. Two basic stages prior to awakening to one's heart or seeing through the mind's illusion (there are vast and varied levels within these stages that overlap based on one's conditioned strengths and weaknesses).

Traits of people in the first stage;

- One is mostly on autopilot, living their life acting and reacting to those around them. They live from their emotions believing whatever they feel no matter how illogical or unsupported their ideas appear.

- Often life does not feel fair. These people will hurt you at times because they themselves are hurting. Subconsciously their attitude may be to hurt you in the hope you will understand the pain they feel. Most often these people have no idea this is what they are doing. Therefore, they aren't aware of the pattern they are caught in.

- These people may be very successful at work. They define themselves by accumulating material possessions.

- They compete with the Jones' next door. In their minds the more they own, the more they are worth. They mistake material worth with self-worth, these are worlds apart. The trap here is that no matter how much they have, they cannot fill that void within, so they accumulate more.

- They run other people down, in an attempt to justify how they are better off on some level. This serves as a momentary distraction. It's like an affirmation that never really scratches that itch, but it's the closest they can get to it so the pattern continues.

- They are self-serving first, often making it appear that they are doing you a favour while they are benefiting the most. They do not often do anything unless they will gain from it on some level.

- They are too busy giving advice rather than taking it.

- They will give advice that often they themselves don't follow.

- They are the exception to the rules everyone else must follow. These rules don't apply in their minds because they feel they are suffering more and are owed more.

- Their problems are worse than everyone else's. Their jobs are harder than even their co-workers.

- They struggle to feel empathy.

- They hold grudges for years.

- They refuse to take responsibility for their emotional state. They'd rather blame anyone or anything else. This not only maintains their suffering but increases it over time.

The second stage (more likely to be reading this book) are looking for more meaning in life. You want to gain some form of control of your life to ease your suffering or the suffering of others. You become hungry for information, eager to get somewhere or to find something and you may try countless methods or techniques in your search for inner peace. Many of these attributes below are offered through courses by others in the second stage. They may even sell an idea or a way to 'short-track' to the next stage of true joy and freedom.

- You become less reactive.

- Things don't affect for you as long.

- Your start to understand others points of view on a deeper level.

- You begin to guide people into themselves instead of blaming everyone else for their suffering. Helping them to start taking responsibility for themselves.

- More people will seek your advice.

- People are more drawn to you.

- You listen on a deeper level.

- You stop interrupting or cutting people off, allowing them to freely express.

- You begin to enjoy silence.

- You begin to seek more out of life and start realising you have a choice in how you think and feel.

Then there's the next phase - awakening to your heart. I believe there is no greater goal than to reach the third stage and beyond.

- You take full responsibility for all your thoughts, feelings and actions.

- You no longer try to control others, rather encouraging them.

- You stop competing with people. You allow them to have their view without needing to prove them wrong.

- You slow down, living in the now moment and no longer avoiding oneself. You know how to nurture yourself, therefore others.

- You condemn no one. You understand very deeply that people's actions are a result of their own suffering and misunderstandings.

- You fully support one's inner journey, rather than trying to control their path, choices and realisations.

- You have realised the illusion of your thoughts and are therefore free from its torment.

- You have become truly free within.

- You have found peace.

My wish is that while you read this book, you reflect and question your own thought patterns. This in turn will enable you to start unravelling the self-defeating patterns in your thinking. By your self-reflection, questioning yourself and developing awareness, you will start to literally rewire your brain. This is a journey to a place of true happiness, peace, wonder and complete self-acceptance. From this space true love resides with the capacity to love and nurture all. You will *naturally* be compassionate, understanding towards yourself and others. You will understand the clear difference between guiding through love and controlling through fear. This does not just apply to our children; this is the basis of all healthy communication!

CHAPTER 1

SILENCE - WHAT WE AVOID IS WHAT WE NEED!

So, WHAT DOES silence give us? The most important thing silence enables us to do is *to become aware of our thoughts and their processes*. This in turn enables us to *question and begin to see through our thoughts*. Without this ability we have no real control of ourselves. We are like a piece of driftwood being washed around at sea. The media, our peers and our environment control us and we get caught in the whole 'emotional play'. We may feel calm at times, but storms will always roll in in one form or another and our ability to focus on what supports our mental, emotional and physical needs may be severely limited because we are believing all those negative thoughts within our minds. When you start developing the ability to question and ultimately see through your thoughts, *you begin to earn your freedom.*

This is a place of deep understanding of yourself and therefore others. You cannot have one without the other, but it always starts inward first and ripples out like a kind of chain reaction or knowing. In this space, if someone tries to hurt or manipulate you, you are able to see a deeper truth. You can see their pain and misunderstanding; it is clear they are trying to survive *their own storm* within. You may just be the closest person they try to grab to pull their head above water.

When there is panic, one is in fight or flight mode; fear rushes in, rationality no longer applies. The greater the fear, the less one is capable of seeing. Reputation (shame) or survival is at stake. Both feelings can be debilitating and limit access to rational thought.

As long as you are blaming another for how you're feeling, you are believing that you have no power to change. You are believing that you are the victim, that unless another changes their attitude, their ways, you cannot change. Luckily, this is absolutely not true!

Here are some simple understandings or tests to reflect on whether you feel you deeply understand yourself and therefore others;

- Do you recommend people should follow in your exact footsteps to find what you have found?

- Do you interrupt others when they open to you to tell them that you know exactly what they mean and start telling your story?

- Do you interrupt when people open to you and tell them your ideas or what they should be doing?

- Do you tell them what everyone else should be doing?

- Are you jumping on board when they blame another?

- Do you justify your views to people, friends or family?

- Do you try to prove you're right and others are wrong?

If you answer yes to all or any of these questions, then you haven't fully discovered your heart yet! When you truly discover the beautiful softness of your heart it encompasses you. You realise your past misunderstandings and struggles. You become compassionate to yourself and others. You will finally ask questions rather than giving *all the answers in an attempt to convince oneself or being self-righteous,* A farmer doesn't tell everyone he's a farmer, or try to prove to everyone that he knows how to farm, or the ins and outs of farming, he just farms!

CHAPTER 2

A CHILDHOOD EXPERIENCE

DURING JACKSON'S YOUNGER *years he was an average guy. He played sport, surfed, rarely spoke of emotions and even more rarely displayed them. He had a minimal religious upbringing. He wasn't interested in going to church. He went to spiritual bands on occasion with his school friends when they came to town (it was an excuse to hang out with mates and check out girls). The bands and religious followers put him off religion by trying to make him feel guilty for not committing to their beliefs. They would say, "The guilt you feel is God calling you." Jackson never understood the people with the view 'This is the one true way'. He always felt, 'what if you were born into Hinduism or Buddhism. Imagine a Buddhist dying and going to God and God says, "I know you have harmed no one, have cultivated love and peace. But unfortunately, you were born in the wrong place and followed the wrong religion. Although you knew nothing about the 'one true religion', that's just a bit of bad luck. Sorry you can't come in."' It didn't make sense.*

Jackson had an amazing experience when he was 17. His football club made the grand final in two grades; Under 17s and men's first grade. He played in the under 17's and they lost. Later that day he played in the second half of the men's first-grade final and his team lost as well. That's certainly not the amazing experience. Jackson was sitting in the pub afterwards with his mates. He raised a beer and was about to take a sip and in a brief moment a feeling of 'I'm a man now' crept into his psyche. That feeling lasted only a moment (he thought he'd made it!). It then dawned on him; **this isn't enough.** *He knew then he needed answers. He knew there had to be much more to life than this. He didn't even take a sip. He placed the glass on the counter, looked around at his mates. Jackson felt like he was in some kind of time warp, observing all those around him, oblivious of his experience. He needed more! He knew then that his journey had just begun. Jackson had no idea where to go or what to do. He only knew that he had to search for some kind of meaning, a purpose.*

Jackson had his ups and downs growing up, with his fair share of emotional turmoil. Watching his parents try to deal with their anger, unmet expectations and frustrations. Trying to escape the momentum of choices they made as young adults, their conditioning. They realised things weren't working and struggled to shield both Jackson and his sister Ava as best they could from their inner turmoil from an early age. This of course is impossible for anyone in pain to achieve. Like all children, Jackson and Ava were very perceptive. They felt everything. Life wasn't all bad but eventually it took its toll on all of them.

By late high school Jackson was angry a lot of the time. He very rarely fought while in school and by high school the tough kids left Jackson alone purely because he took no crap playing football.

Jackson played football for 22 years. He started playing from age 9 to impress his dad and to seek acceptance. At first, he was afraid but then he soon discovered another side to him while playing football. By late high school, football was all he cared about. Jackson mostly tried to do the right thing in school and life in general. He rarely swore, was popular because of his sporting prowess and he got along with everyone. He didn't like conflict and always tried to avoid it. He was the quiet, polite type and suppressed all his negative emotions.

During his senior years of high school his parents were going through their toughest times. Jackson spent a lot of time looking out the window at school and his mind became foggy as he tried to detach from the turmoil he felt. This other side to Jackson was a hurting, very angry and tough young man with a lot of attitude and football was his lifeline. This is where he felt he earned respect. He never ever backed down. Always played fair, but hard. He'd go out there and try to break the opposition in half. If someone played dirty, he went after them. It was a legal battlefield. It was the outlet he needed, and the one place he felt he had control. Jackson was fast and strong. The football field was the one place he could face his fears.

Before his senior years in high school, Jackson did really well. He did advanced maths and even received 90% in a half yearly maths exam. Two years later at the start of one of his final exams, Jackson had to write his name and his teacher's name. He'd had her for two years and for the life of him he couldn't remember her name. After 10 minutes he thought "It's either Mrs. Richards or Mrs. Richardson, I'm just going to have to take a guess". What made things worse and compounded the pressure was that she tutored him once a week for the year leading up to the exam! She was kind and compassionate, he really liked her. He was thinking "She's going to think I'm an idiot", and was struggling to hold it together. Not your ideal start to a final exam. Jackson felt, 'I might as well walk out now'. Jackson failed the exam. He dreaded receiving his results in the mail and when they arrived, he had to muster all his courage to open it. He wanted to say it was lost in the mail. He wasn't expecting much but it was worse than he could have imagined. From that moment on Jackson felt the only chance he had in life was through football. Being able to channel his anger during his senior years at high school allowed him to stand out enough to represent his state playing football. He went on an 18-day tour representing his state and his team was undefeated. His team won the championships but unfortunately Jackson perforated his eardrum in a game before the final.

Due to Jackson's unresolved anger, over time he felt he deserved any pain he received while playing. There was an internal war within him that would make him play even harder, but no matter how hard he tried or whatever level he reached, it was never enough. Jackson never felt whole. He felt there was always something lacking. He didn't care if he hurt himself as long as the opposition were hurting more. By his mid-20's some of his team mates said he was like a kamikaze because he had no self-preservation. Jackson has played football with a damaged rib cartilage, a broken hand, concussion, and a torn cartilage in his shoulder, torn tissue in his shoulder joint and in a semi-final, he fractured his jaw in two places, went off the field only to return for a period in the second half. All to try to prove he was a man; failure was not an option. He played representative football for 3 years from 1990 to 92. In 1993 he made the all-star country team and later received a contract to play professionally in 1995.

On one occasion when starting a training session in a local gym with a mate, Jackson was doing power training, power snatches where the idea is to approach the bar, then explode from a power lift to a full extension over his head. He finished his first set and decided to go for his record lift the next set. He almost made it. The bar was over his head. He was straining to fully extend his arms, then **pop***! Jackson's right shoulder popped out of joint and the bar crashed down behind him with an almighty* **bang***. This drew his mate's attention, lucky no one else was around. He came over and said, "Wow, look at the lump on your shoulder". Jackson looked down and realised it was out of joint. He looked around and saw a bench, walked over, grabbed hold* *and pulled it back into place. Moments later the team trainer walked in. He asked, "What have you been doing?" Jackson casually eased over to an exercise bike, hopped on and said, "I'm just warming down after a session." The beads of sweat rolling down Jackson's face from the injury would have fooled even the keenest eye. That weekend during his game he went to stop a big forward from running past him with the same shoulder and he ran through him like a turnstile, popping it out again. Jackson laid on his back, popped it in again and played on. Frustration and injuries limited his footy aspirations, every time he was on the brink of an opportunity to cement a position he was injured. Life had something else in stall for Jackson.*

As you have read, just like many men, Jackson tried to prove he was a man by his deeds, some very stupid. Not one of these deeds brought him closer to that goal. Jackson had been seeking self-worth his entire life. He looked to others for a sense of worth because he had little. He questioned his intuition (his gut feeling) over another's. That is not living. He felt alone, hollow, only when everything was slipping away from his grip, did he realise that his integrity is the only thing he couldn't live without. In the end he risked everything to get it back.

Through Jackson's 20s he went through a number of significant changes. At 21, he went through a depression. During this time, one evening he was laying on his bed, contemplating, reflecting and trying to rationalise a way through this suffering. He spoke to God. "God, my life is not my own, I'm suffering and there's nothing I can do. I've tried but I've failed." Then it hit him… he had the answer. "God let me serve you." He was an open book and he had no idea where this would lead, but it made sense to support or trust that which supports all life (surely there can be no greater joy). From that day on his life began taking a huge turn, like a massive ship gradually changing course for new lessons and opportunities. But the fastest way forward is through the roughest seas. exploring the deepest depths of our soul, everything must be stripped bare. Little did he know, in the far-off distance beyond the horizon he was to be tested. If he survived, he would never be the same!

Jackson, amongst his suffering and pain became more open to the realm of possibilities. He started believing at times (even amidst his suffering mind) that he was in the right place at the right time. He trusted on some level that he was being guided. That there were things he needed to discover, to unravel. He discovered meditation and different types of healing, although it wasn't something he always practiced.

Jackson had a dog (Zeus) he really cared for. This was his catalyst into a discovery into his healing potential. When Zeus was less than a year old, he became ill with the Parvovirus. The connection was such that the only way the vet could coerce his dog to another pen was by using the scent from one of Jackson's shirts. Jackson would visit him morning and evening at his vets. One evening on a visit with Zeus, he noticed a large lump on the top right of Zeus' head. Upon examination the vet concluded that if the lump got any larger, he'd have to drill in to drain the area. Jackson was left alone with his dog. He was feeling overwhelmed and disheartened. Then seemingly out of the blue, without much thought, Jackson put both hands on the lump. Suddenly Jackson no longer found himself at the vets. He was looking through the eyes of an eagle flying high above a beautiful valley. He was lost in the captivation of the experience. He had never before felt such overwhelming peace.

Although it felt like only a minute of a profoundly life changing experience, Jackson had spent 15 minutes in a trance like state. On coming to, when Jackson opened his eyes and removed his hands, the lump on his dog was gone. He called the vet nurse. On seeing the change, she rushed away in denial of what had just transpired. While patting his dog, Jackson noticed his hand heat up over the area he had just healed. This was the very beginning of Jackson's healing journey and as the years passed, Jackson learned, developed and discovered many ways to apply healing on himself and others.

In Jackson's 30s he was going through family court trying to resolve and reach settlement, all while running a business and finishing a home that he and his ex-wife designed. They had two children together. At the time the final trial was on the horizon he had been making decisions through fear of losing and settling for less than he wanted rather than following what felt right within his heart. From the outset it looked bad. As a result, both his ex-partners were saying he was crazy, needed help and his sanity was being questioned. Even though these points were being raised, along with the prospect of Jackson not seeing his kids, he knew in the end he'd rather be alone and whole than have everything and be broken.

Seeking approval, fear of conflict, making bad decisions through fear of losing his kids, his business and his reputation almost destroyed Jackson. It doesn't have to get to that. You don't have to go without anything. But you must prioritise. To learn to truly live your life and love your life you must first and foremost be true to you. As you will discover in the pages to follow, living a lie is not living at all.

CHAPTER 3

ROUGHEST SEAS

Sometime's in one's life, one has to be stripped back to bare nothing to discover what remains.

This was Jackson's journey; 'Some lights will only be seen on the darkest of nights.'

Obstacles told to Jackson in his late 30's that he began to believe;

"You're a crazy person."
"Your personality changed 15 times in the last half hour."
"You need to go to a mental hospital."
"You need medication."
"Without me you would be in a mental facility on medication."
"Anyone that sees you on the street can see you are mentally ill."
"You are a compulsive liar."
"You are volatile."
"You have a personality disorder."
"You are abusive."
"You deserved the physical abuse."
"Without me you will lose your kids."

One of the most traumatic moments of Jackson's life was late 2009. He was running around with his kids. He picked them up during the week and dropped his kids off on the Friday. Early the following week he was informed that something wasn't right with his daughter Able, that she'd shut down. He asked what was going on and he was told nothing. Jackson had trouble sleeping that night. He rang back after he finished work the next evening. He was told she was with guests so she couldn't speak, but he demanded to know what was going on. It was mentioned that it'd be explained on the weekend. Jackson was asked to take his kids to school on Friday so he did. As they walked into school, one of the parents said hi to his daughter, but gave him the cold shoulder. Jackson kind of knew her so it took him aback. He felt strange at the school and he had no idea why. It seemed people received him in a different way. He left the school feeling something wasn't right.

Later that day when his kids were at their mothers, she rang Jackson and asked him to come and get them for their weekend together. When he arrived, she was on the phone. He waited awhile and when he went to beckon the kids in the car she finally hung up. She went to Jackson and told him "You're not going to like this". She told a story about their kids playing at her friends. "Able and her friend were playing with dolls. The girl's father walked in and said to our daughter", "How do you know if it's a boy doll or a girl doll?" At this point Jackson wanted to jump in his car and pay the bastard a visit, but he listened on, and he didn't know whom her friends were. Then everything felt twisted. According to these parents his daughter made a comment about Jackson. From here his mind became hazy, he failed to comprehend all he'd heard. Before he could get a handle on the situation, Jackson discovered that the father mentioned and his family had literally just moved to China. Jackson's wife said that they reported it to child protection. It appeared everyone had spoken about it. The school and everyone knew about it. Everyone but Jackson! His entire world turned upside down. None of this made sense to him, the way it all transpired. He could not imagine a more malicious attack.

For Jackson nothing gets lower than this. He was broken. He lost interest in the one and only thing that kept him going after he and his ex-broke up a few years earlier, work. Just before Christmas break 2009, he arranged a meeting with his kids' teachers and their principle. He was concerned how the accusations may affect his children. Jackson mentioned in the meeting he didn't want his kids being isolated or not invited anywhere from fear of 'their father'. He mentioned to the principle that if it does impact them, they will change schools. He was shocked at the principal's response. She told Jackson in front of everyone, "The other schools will find out about you as well." He was lost for words; he felt a sense of hopelessness. An accused man is a condemned man!

On leaving the pointless meeting an hour after closing time, Jackson saw his kids in the park with their mum on the way back to his car. He thought they would have been home by then. Upon seeing him they ran over. It was the previous weekend when he arrived at their home, only to leave without them. They ran and embraced their dad. They didn't want to leave. Jackson knew he had to follow protocol until he was cleared to have them, so he encouraged them to go with their mother, but they refused. One of the parents and Jackson's ex-wife's mum had to drag his son Logan away. His daughter Able had to be pulled from Jackson as she refused to let go. She scratched the back of Jacksons neck while screaming and trying to hold on. Once they were free from Jackson he turned around and walked toward his car, tears streaming down his cheeks. He could not bear to see them in such turmoil. Amidst their despair there was nothing he could do. They told him later they feared they would never see him again.

Jackson was cleared of the accusations and started seeing his kids again. But all his negative thoughts intensified from here on and he stopped paying attention to his life. When you take your eyes off the ball someone else starts running with it. The wolves were at his door. He didn't notice his accountant ripping off tens of thousands of dollars from his business and in the end he had so many hands in his pockets looking for a payout that he didn't know whom half of them belonged to. His life spiraled out of control leading to bad choices, not seeing his kids for a year whilst being in an intense relationship and losing his company through liquidation. paedophilia is probably the only accusation that even when innocent, most people will always consider one guilty. Why take the chance? For the sake of his children he wouldn't. Jackson felt condemned as he has condemned others. A disturbing fact is that there are predators out there that don't get caught. Unfortunately, some will throw that very serious accusation around purely to hurt others.

Jackson became emotionally and mentally weak, feeling like he was broken. He had a friend Annie, whom at that time emotionally supported him and was a shoulder to cry on. He felt extremely lost and confused and had lost all motivation. Jackson felt very alone and had a lot of fear around relationships. In spite of this, he fell into one with Annie about three years after breaking up with his ex-wife. He became dependent on her. He stopped trusting himself, his intuition, feeling too encased in turmoil. This was the start of the most horrendous and intense few years of his life and his greatest journey. If he'd seen the path he was destined to travel ahead of him, he would have done anything to avoid it. The journey to discover who we are, that emanating light within, feels absolutely impossible when we are encased in turmoil with the feeling of no way out.

The residue from the aftermath of the shocking accusations toward Jackson had a subtle, yet undeniable retributional feel, that haunted him for a period. Then one day, seemingly out of nowhere it dawned on Jackson. Only months prior, whilst talking to his good mate Terrence, he was asked after a previous traumatic time concerning the emotional well being of his kids; if his father-in-law may have had 'access' to his daughter. Jackson objected initially as he had good relations with his father-in-law at that time. But after Terrence explained how often 'things' happen within family, a shred of doubt arose.

Jackson mentioned this possibility to his ex-wife, not in an accusational tone but more concerned and perplexed. It still wasn't something Jackson wanted to believe. As one would expect, it wasn't received well. Jackson did not pursue this, there was no follow up, there was no proof, just doubt planted by a mate.

From this moment on, whilst still being separated, everything changed within both sides of the family dynamic. There was a clear and obvious coldness or harshness. Only a few months later, Jackson found himself on the receiving end of this far greater and grievous attack.

There is a part of Jackson in all of us, we have all lived his journey to varying degrees.

Poetry is a great catalyst in accessing the depths of our pain, fear or a sense of hopelessness that many of us will experience at some point in our lives. If we are willing and have the courage, it will enable a greater perspective and understanding of not only ourselves, but those around us.

This may feel terrifying, yet is a crucial alternative to turning a blind eye. Lancing the wound, exposing pain in all its rawness can really accelerate our healing journey. It's important to ensure we do this in a safe and nurturing environment.

I was not always as I am now. I too have been buried deeply in misery off and on over the years seeking peace and the end of my suffering mind.

I have written a number of poems over the years from the first time I went to India soul searching in 2002. I had thought they were all lost, but while digging through some old boxes, I found buried deep in an old book of mine, some of the poetry I had written whilst in the depths of my despair over the course of a few years.

I apologise for the language but they are original and very raw, and reveal the despair and how lost I had felt at times. I've decided to add them below as an inspiration to those who have suffered or are still suffering.

As you will begin to see as you continue to read my book. There IS a way through your suffering. As it was for me, it can be for you. As you read on, I will reveal to you my insights and tempt you on your own journey to self-discovery.

Remember, never give in, there is always a way forward, there is always hope!

Rage

Aaaarrrrrrghhhh
I want to shake something
Fucking break something
You want to beat me
You can't defeat me
You abuse me
Fucking accuse me
You trash my name
The games you play
I'm not to blame
It's just your way
Go fuck yourself
Is what I say
You've crossed the line
And awakened the lion
Now hear me roar
And prepare to fall
Feel the fire
You fucking liar
Of the life you conceal
All will be revealed
I swear!

Suffering Mind

Fear to go beyond
Acknowledge the truth
Realisation of past failures
A once pure and clean fabric

(Or so I thought)
Is now full of holes and loose ends
Holding up to the light
The purity of the sun reveals all the imperfections
Interwoven into my mind
Beyond repair it can conceal no more
Not even to my eyes
I see the many coloured patches and misconceptions
My children's pain and the loved ones around me
Years of being alone
Avoiding that which is upon me
Thinking all where better off without me
And me them
Life has other ideas
Revealing what I was afraid to see
So many flaws…
Reflecting on my childhood
Deep sadness, anger, frustration
Looking for acceptance, love
Why wasn't I seen?
No one to rescue me
We all want the same
To be loved, nurtured
As I nurture the child within
The more clearly I see the pain in my children's eyes
Wanting to be rescued
Reaching out to me
Connecting more each time
The pain grows each time I let them go
A promise for a better life
With no short term fix
Sits heavy in all our hearts

A mother too encased in her own suffering
Cannot see her children's
Constant refusal to look in one's own direction
Creates pain and breaks hearts all around
Throwing salt on my past
This is my Karma
But it will not be my children's

Inner Turmoil

For so long I've been wandering these baron lands within me
For so long I have thirsted
At times even swam in the river of life
So much water all around
Yet I am never quenched
Maybe I do not truly know how to drink
Once again I happen to an oasis
Once again I search
Not knowing what I'm looking for
A spark of life
A reason to exist
A driving force
Through the many miracles I've seen and done
Fearless in adversity
Yet fearing myself
Surrounded by darkness in a clear blue sky
Waves of emotion hit me
Submerge me
Swallow me
At times I gulp for air

At times I drift
Allowing the darkness within to drag me to the bottom
Alone I sit
Wondering when I will return
This place is so familiar
My dark haven
Too deep for many to reach
Nothing here but misery
Consumed by darkness
Its afraid to let me go
After many years of service
It fights for its survival
Slowly it feeds from me
Sapping my strength
How do I swim to escape
With so little fuel!
Then I feel it
Building within me
A once dormant force of raw untapped power
Building with every breath
A rage I have suppressed
Coursing within my veins
A side of me I feared
Now may save me...
How can light come from darkness?
A raw destructive power
Leaves fear its wake
And respect
Fights for love
And truth

A spark of life
The balance is within me
At last I have fight
Now I can be whole

The Divine

From a distance I hear your constant call
So close to my heart
Ever so subtle
Beckoning me

CHAPTER 4

BROKEN

L OOKING AT HOW it got to the point of Jackson not seeing his kids for a year and having supervised visits should be a great lesson for anyone reading on. He made more than his fair share of mistakes as many of us have, to the point of losing everything. All the things most of us use to define success, he lost. The more he altered his choices through fear of losing certain benchmarks the more it led to him losing them anyway. What made things far worse and what hurt Jackson the most during his downward spiral, was that he lost his integrity, his truth, his heart. The bottom line is, this is all you can ever truly have. The rest is hollow, fleeting! Given all the things on this Earth, heart and honesty within, is by far is the most important to us. The beautiful thing is, when these aspects line up, so does everything else. Unfortunately, almost no one can truly let go long enough, to find this out. Regardless of this fact, life will loosen our grip on what we think we know and what we think is real over time.

Jackson had a great teacher, his partner Annie. Each fortnight while with his kids, they would be pretty clingy with him. Sometimes they'd fight to sit on his lap on the lounge if they were about to watch a movie. They were still pretty young and clingy. Chloe missed out on this opportunity with her father as a child, so understandably this brought up some pain for both Annie and her daughter Chloe. After the weekend with their dad, when Logan and Able returned to their mothers, Jackson would feel sad and irritable at seeing his kids go. Annie felt the same due to her child. So, after many weekends with Jackson's kids he and Annie would argue. He didn't like conflict and learned from an early age to clam up and conform. Through no fault of his kids, he began to feel uneasy when he saw them around Annie. He felt he couldn't fully be himself, or that Logan or Able could be either, otherwise it would often end in conflict for everyone. He felt compromised, and just as he thought the situation couldn't get any worse, it did. Annie began physically abusing Jackson, oftentimes in front of her daughter, Chloe. It wasn't the physical abuse that was most debilitating, he was strong and could take a hit, it was the ridicule he felt in front of Annie and Chloe, feeling squashed, abused and worthless.

Annie attacked him physically, mentally and emotionally. Oftentimes during these episodes Chloe would scream at Jackson, "Don't hurt my mom." Jackson never understood until years later why she would say that. She feared at some point during the abuse that one day he'd strike her back. Jackson never did. Jackson called the police on two occasions during these abusive attacks for a reprieve, so he could get some space as Annie and her daughter were living with him. Jackson kept spare clothes in his car as a precaution, in case he needed a quick escape. His environment was unpredictable.

One day Jackson was given an ultimatum by Annie; he was told to not see his kids for a while and to seek professional help. Annie believed Jackson's mental state was the reason they weren't getting along. He was also told that his kids took him for granted and that if he stopped seeing them, they would appreciate him more in the future.

Pressure was also dramatically added on the work front for Jackson as he ran his own business. Not too long before Annie's ultimatum, he was called to one of his worksites one morning by the union. He went with Terrence. They met quite a few years ago while doing security work together in Sydney. When they arrived on site the union boss told Jackson that his company was breaking the law and that if he called the Office of the Construction Commission he would go to jail. That afternoon he had a meeting with a number of union officials and one of their lawyers at their office building.

They demanded $700,000 by the next morning or else they would close Jackson's business. Jackson walked out of the building thinking he was going into liquidation. At that time things were very tight financially with his business. He didn't have anywhere near that sort of money. The next morning the union arrived at two of Jackson's main work sites in the city. They put fear into his workers by telling them it was unlawful for them to work. Jackson couldn't blame the guys for not working because at that point he was also intimidated by the union officials.

A government task force became involved and Jackson was informed the union were being unlawful in their actions. Back at his office, he started going over his records and as he looked, he started noticing discrepancies. He asked for his admin to print a copy of all the payments to his accountant. She said there was only one payment in the system. He then recalled, a year or so prior, his accountant 'accidentally' wiped his company's office program while working from his office. The accountant said he could restore it but obviously only partially did. Around the same time as this realisation, the taxation office sent a letter saying Jackson's company owed around $1.6 million in taxes as they had never been paid. He was panic stricken. His system had holes through it and he wasn't sure he could trace everything. Jackson had paid tax direct to the ATO and also to the accountant for the tax *department as requested by his accountant. He then realised he'd been had by his accountant.*

Amongst all these dramas, one of his workers were attempting to take him to court chasing money. Jackson had meetings with additional lawyers to appear in a specific wage court tribunal with the union who represented him. This guy ended up being fined by the court for his actions.

Another four workers had a case against Jackson according to a government body and he went to court to defend this too. He was currently under the microscope due to the union. There appeared to be a battle between the union and the government, of which Jackson was caught in the crossfire. He knew if he couldn't resolve this soon, he would surely lose everything. Although the writing seemed on the wall, for now Jackson was still kicking. His lawyers were trying to get files from his accountant to give the correct information to the taxation department. This, after letters and many phone calls, failed.

Jackson went to see his new accountants as appointed by the court. He was told that around $800,000 was unreconciled from the business (wiped by his previously accountant), that if it remained it would be assumed Jackson took it and the worst-case scenario is that he would go to jail.

Under the circumstances Jackson's vulnerabilities became more apparent in his relationship. Jackson would never have considered not seeing his kids, not even for a short time. But under all these circumstances and Annie's advice, he made the choice not to see his kids for a short period. Jackson started seeing a psychologist (Jones), as recommended by Annie. She described Jackson to Jones as angry, volatile and a pathological liar with mood swings, to name just a few traits.

On all these visits he barely said a word. He never mentioned being physically abused or the lack of control he felt in their relationship. Jones never saw Jackson one on one and based his assessment on everything Annie told him. Jackson feared where this was leading.

Jackson was prescribed two types of medication; a mood stabilizer and an antidepressant. As expected, when his ex-wife caught wind of the situation, she requested confirmation through her lawyers from psychologist Jones, that their kids were safe with him. In Jones' first letter he failed to address this point. He stated that Jackson had (based on Annie's view) a 'Cluster B' personality disorder. This was a complete shock to him. He never saw it coming as Jones never shared his view or diagnosis before this time. This all seemed very extreme. With everything that was going on in Jackson's life, he was becoming more and more broken and depressed. This resulted in his medication going up. He was walking around feeling detached and disheartened. Around this time began his fight to see his kids amidst all the other obstacles in his life.

Two weeks following the first psychiatric report he forwarded a second letter stating that there was no risk to his children. His ex-wife challenged this letter and his lawyer felt she had a right to question this also. Jackson was shocked. He felt abandoned by his lawyers. They had been representing him for quite a while. They were well aware of the misdirection's and unanswered letters from his ex-wife, which gave them the feeling of unaccountability and a sense of 'doing what one pleases', as previously expressed by his lawyers. Jackson stressed to his lawyers his disapproval, but it was too late. They had already responded to Jacksons ex-wife without his consent.

Throughout Jackson's life he had been around and handled intense situations. He worked in security for four years and he was Head Doorman for a while and worked alone at various establishments in major cities. He had certainly been in challenging situations and had escorted numerous people outside over the years due to unruly behaviour. Even while in a physically abusive relationship, Jackson had never struck out or harmed anyone. He always saw himself as a protector. He had a clean record. He couldn't believe that now he was being treated as though he was an abuser.

Often a war ensues when both parents disagree and are in pain. It becomes more about winning than what's best for their kids. After a while sometimes we can't even remember what we are fighting for. Just that we are at war and we fight for every inch, giving away nothing at the cost of everyone's expense, including our own. We have all made decisions we regret. Unchecked emotional turmoil, pain and the feeling of no control is to blame, not the underlying beautiful hearts of those partaking in this experience. People often vent their heightened emotional state during these times, but it's not to be mistaken for reality or truth. Not to be totally disregarding but it's mostly an expression of pain, suffering within and projection. In this space we not only remind ourselves of the pain and suffering but exaggerate and intensify it, absorbing the numerous fear-based possibilities that we would not previously have ever considered.

This is not about judgements; it's about understanding the pain we inflict on ourselves and one another.

In Jackson's final Family Court hearing in 2012 on the first day, his lawyers strongly recommended he conform to his ex-wife's demands of having 25 sessions with a clinical psychologist followed by a potential minimum 6 sessions with a psychiatrist. In the meantime, he was to pay for supervised visits with his children each fortnight. The lawyers said Jackson could 'prove her wrong' with a clean bill of mental health.

Little was he to know, in the court's eyes and in their final assessment, they viewed his agreement to be assessed as an admission to having mental health issues. No doubt Jackson's lawyers would have known this, yet it was not conveyed.

Jackson broke up with Annie at Christmas in 2011 during another altercation with her. Jackson called the police after more abuse. They arrived and Jackson asked them to stay while he packed a few things so he could leave without any further abuse.

Prior to Jackson breaking up with Annie and before his final trial with his ex-wife, he saw another psychiatrist on his own to get some grounding and perspective on everything he was experiencing. His back was against the wall with the feeling of multiple walls crashing in on him. Jackson told him all he'd been going through including his vast experiences with Annie. He left nothing out. After two visits and a literal head scan from a clinic, he cleared Jackson and refused to see him any further as he identified no personality disorders. Prior to Christmas 2011 Jackson had been assessed by three independent psychiatrists and had sessions with a clinical psychologist as well as being in and out of court with work and family court.

In another court hearing late in 2011, Jackson and his lawyers negotiated a company fine and personal fine due to negligence (Jackson's lack of knowledge regarding subcontractors cost him). Jackson always gave his worker's a choice of being an employee or a subcontractor and had a combination of both the entire time he was operating. He discovered this wasn't technically correct or lawful. There was supposed to be a distinguishable difference in duties. Despite this, he thought, 'Finally I'm slowly coming out the other end of my dramas'. There was little time for reflection. Next Jackson had a call from his lawyers regarding payroll tax.

It appeared he owed the ATO more money. This would ultimately sink his company.

Late in 2011, Jackson's family lawyers were recommending that Annie agreed to supervise him with his children so he could start gaining access to them again. His lawyers called to speak with Annie on several occasions, but after some arguing between them she stuck by her guns. She explained to Jackson that if she agreed, it would not look good on Jacksons record as he does not need supervision. Annie disregarded this very point only two months later.

Jackson's ex-wife had been listening in on every phone call with his kids for a long time. After the accusation of paedophilia in late 2009 and the blame laid upon him for any trouble she experienced with their kids, Jackson questioned his kid's health under her care. Logan and Able became very self-conscious in all their communications. He had been pushing through his lawyers for an independent evaluation to make sure they were doing okay, but his ex-wife kept refusing this. Finally, the assessment happened around Christmas 2011.

When Jackson first walked into the office of the assessing psychologist Smith, one of his first questions was, "How do you feel about being here today?" Jackson responded, "I've been trying to organise this assessment for two years so I feel good." Smith told him there was three versions of the story; both parents' versions and finally there is his version, "The truth".

If someone ever tells you this, *run*! It's a ridiculous statement. There can only ever be four versions in this situation. The fourth version of course is the truth which cannot be known by anyone but God (the silent witness). Interpretations are relative and will always fall short (especially when emotions are involved). Needless to say, in context to this chapter, things didn't go Jackson's way.

Psychologist Smith mentioned in a later report for court that no psychologist could make an accurate assessment after just two sessions (with the exception of himself of course), disregarding a report from the psychologist whom Jackson saw twice on his own, gave him a literal head scan and wrote there was no personality disorder. Interestingly enough, after one session, Smith was the only person to say Jackson needed to be supervised and for a whopping two years by Annie. Jackson received Smiths report stating his findings in December 2011. He couldn't believe it. After Annie had read it, realising she had been recommended to supervise Jackson for a whopping two years, her initial response was, "Yay, now we can get married!" Her view of how supervised visits looked had now been superseded. This didn't sit well with Jackson at all. He and Annie fought often throughout their relationship and it was getting worse. The thought of being in this environment ongoing was too much for him to bear. He was on medication and was allowing himself to be controlled.

From 2010, Jackson slowly became more and more cut off from the world. He stopped playing sports which he loved, he rarely went out or exercised. He was told by Annie that he was only doing it to gain attention from females (just feeding his ego). Jackson went from 93kg and pretty fit to 112kg in no time. If he was out with Annie and she felt some other women was vying for his attention she would say to him, "Go to the car and wait for me." There were some places Jackson wasn't allowed to go back to. He became extremely self-conscious. He started believing there was something really wrong with him. He doubted his intuition. He doubted everything about himself. He started feeling that he was the cause of everyone's problems.

On one occasion coming back from a nice weekend away, Jackson, Annie and her daughter Chloe stopped at Pemberton. Annie believed Jackson was trying to gain attention from a waitress at the cafe. Once they got back to the car and were driving off, Annie started going crazy.

She started abusing Jackson and had numerous fits of uncontrolled rage, hitting him many times in the face while he was driving up to speeds of 100km per hour. Meanwhile Chloe was screaming and crying on the back seat, fearful of having a collision. By the time they arrived home Jackson had a black eye and blood had ran down to his chin after she had slowly poked him with her fingernail in the side of his cheek while he was driving. Jackson had a psychologist appointment with Psychologist Jones (the one that diagnosed he had a Cluster B personality disorder based on Annie's views) the very next day. Jackson was convinced by Annie it was in his best interest to postpone this appointment until he had healed. Looking back, it'd be hard for many to imagine why he agreed. Jackson was trying to minimise confrontation in his abusive home life.

By Christmas 2011 reflecting over the past year, from where Jackson was standing and more so where he was heading, he felt extremely depressed. He felt more and more buried in this situation and the hole was just getting deeper. Jackson had been in fear for so much of the year that he became too afraid to follow his truth, that integrity within. He was too worried about his reputation, how others would perceive him and what more he could possibly lose. When everything is threatened the easiest choice to make is what looks to be the safest, and Jackson went against his gut feeling, leading him into even more turmoil. In the end Jackson was feeling so lost, he was unsure he could ever find his way back. Projecting into the future of what his safe but hollow life might look like gave him a sense of complete hopelessness. He had stopped listening to his inner voice, his intuition. He felt he was living a lie within. This was not living at all. He felt dead inside.

While trying to piece everything together Jackson started picking up a few discrepancies around him. The most predominant one was the switch from Annie choosing not to supervise him because it wasn't in Jackson's best interest to now, 'who cares because now we can get married!' He started wondering what other discrepancies there were and questioning where he was putting his trust. Jackson was at a point where he believed he couldn't see clearly at all. He was broken and vulnerable. He remembered saying to psychologist Jones at the end of a visit after listening to Annie speak about him, "There must be something seriously wrong with me, I have no recollection of the things she's saying, nothing. I must have a split personality."

By December 2011 Annie and Jackson's arguing intensified. At times she would walk away saying, "What would you know, you're a crazy person." Jackson was feeling completely overwhelmed, worthless and he seriously doubted himself. He knew that if he didn't work out soon what was true within him, it might be too late. Jackson had his final Family Court trial scheduled for January 11th 2012, or so he thought. Annie told him if he didn't go along with what she was saying he would lose his kids, that without her this would surely happen.

Jackson was becoming desperate. He needed to work out what was real, which way to turn, if he was crazy and imagining things or not. He was still on medication at the time and because he questioned his memory recall, he realised the only way to see if he could trust his feelings or intuition was to write a step by step account of life as it happened. The next thing he had to work out was how to do this and keep it hidden from Annie. For a while now she had full access to all his emails, computers and phone. She had access to absolutely everything in Jackson's life, successfully cutting him off from all his friends and family. He was completely alienated.

Annie had messaged Jacksons ex-wife from his phone on several occasions. She assumed it was Jackson (naturally) and some of the messages served as evidence against him in court. Some of the correspondence between his ex-wife and Annie he was aware of, some not. There were times Jackson would walk outside and leave Annie to it.

Due to Annie accessing Jackson's phone and at times deleting things, he came up with an idea of how to hide his writing during his evaluation of himself, in a notepad app on his phone titled 'Last Pay'. Jackson often tracked his workers hours on his phone. It was the safest option. From his step by step account over the next week of what he felt and experienced (documenting everything immediately after it occurred), he realised that everything he felt was real. Finally, he could begin trusting his intuition again. Jackson had found a crucial piece of himself. From that moment on he knew he had to get out!

It was the afternoon of the 2nd of January 2012 when Jackson called the police after an argument and abusive afternoon with his partner. He waited for them to arrive so he could pack and finally leave without further incident. The following morning, Jackson had a call from his lawyers. They received an email from Annie saying he was suicidal. She informed them that all correspondence was to go through her as he wasn't himself. Jackson replied to his lawyers, "I have not felt better in a very long time." A massive weight had been taken from his shoulders. As the Family Court date drew closer, he started receiving emails and calls from his lawyers informing him that Annie had written numerous emails to psychologist Jones and Jackson's ex-wife about his current state of mind. Under the circumstances it was strongly recommended he didn't show in court by his lawyers. This resulted in an adjournment to late March 2012. In court on the 11th January it was ruled that Jackson could not go within 100m of his kid's school, or have any contact with them until the next court date.

After all the dramas he had experienced over the past year he at least felt some relief and breathing space from being single again.

In the month of his trial Jackson discovered that Annie had teamed up with his ex-wife in court. Annie had previously pointed out how it would look in court for Jackson, going against the grain in his choices and stopping his medication. At that point he'd realised going with the grain was destroying him and going with what others thought he should do almost led to his demise. Living another's truth can never fill that void within us. This was one of Jackson's greatest teachings. Finally, he was going his way, irrespective of how it looked to the outside world. He had never felt so free his entire life. An indication to Jackson that things had truly changed within, was an experience he felt for the first time. This was during a phone call with someone that was often passive aggressive toward him. They made a remark toward him and his children whom were wanting to see him.

Passive aggression was an area Jackson always had trouble dealing with. It is likened to someone stepping on our toe. We look the other way and do not speak up in case we offend or disrespect them, even though they're hurting and disrespecting us. Failing to speak up comes down to a lack of self-worth.

Now for the first time in his life, Jackson felt a fire burning within. He didn't get a chance to express himself at the time because they hung up the call, but that fire he felt in his belly was the fire of self-worth. That choice he made against the grain (that fight for survival), against all odds, risking everything, ignited something. He knew then that he had truly discovered something amazing within, something he had never felt before; his inner fire, once truly lit, would never go out.

Not long following this experience Jackson had a second assessment with psychologist Smith appointed by the court to assess his family, whom Jackson originally initiated. Jackson walked in with his new found sense of self, the burden of needing acceptance from everyone felt almost completely diminished. He had been bathing in his new found sense of self-worth since that phone call, therefore he wasn't concerned with his evaluation.

Smith wrote his evaluation on Jackson. Smith was clearly incapable of recognising true insight, an epiphany or change within others. This is evident in 'point 14' of his evaluation of Jackson for court as follows:

"14. On the clinical reassessment Jackson presented as very calm, philosophical and reflective. In the circumstance of the case, I thought that it was an unnaturally normal presentation. It was not the sort of normal presentation of someone masking a clinical depression, rather it was more in keeping with someone who has disconnected from the emotion of the situation which would be more on a personality dysfunction domain."

The other psychologist Jones, whom Jackson only saw with Annie also presented an affidavit for court including information from actual emails written to him by Annie (after they had separated in early January 2012), they were not factual or even tested. How could he possibly know whether she was telling the truth, without knowing the full extent of Jacksons situation? He only received her side of the story from day one.

In court in March 2012 (Jackson's final settlement trial) the magistrate surprised him. The first thing he did was pick up an affidavit from Annie written four months prior while they were still together and read that he was a loving father. He picked up the affidavit, held it in the air, looked at Jacksons ex-wife's barrister and asked, "I don't see anything negative in here, do you?" Her barrister then responded, "No, Your Honour." The Magistrate then asked if Annie was the devil reincarnated as there were two very conflicting affidavits written by her within four months.

Court was settled within one day. Jackson's parents were there. By late morning they were in a room with his barrister. His share of the settlement was around $20K. Jackson's barrister advised him to go along with his ex-wife's request to have supervised visits with his children until all the assessments where completed. This entailed 25 sessions with a clinical psychologist followed by five sessions with a psychiatrist. Jackson was advised by his lawyers at the time that this was only if the clinical psychologist advised him he needed sessions with a psychiatrist. Jackson also knew that if he didn't resolve court in one day he would be walking away with debt and he may still have to go through the same process in the future (on completion of his assessments). His barrister calculated that he had eaten up around $7K of the $20K so Jackson would be walking away with around $13K.

Little did he know, after the court documents were drawn up and the money was transferred into the holding account, Jackson was to walk away with debt. He called his lawyers after a couple of weeks and asked where the remaining money was. They informed him it was all gone and he owed them another $8K. During the phone conversation Jackson was asked how work was going. He responded, "What the hell has that got to do with anything? I told you before things are slow." He then decided to represent himself from here on. It felt as though every hoop that had been thrown at Jackson, he had jumped through while they represented him and did nothing. He felt he could jump through hoops on his own without paying someone else to watch.

By August 2012 his company went into liquidation. By Christmas he filed for bankruptcy. He'd be lying if he said he wasn't a little satisfied he didn't have to pay his family lawyers the outstanding $8K.

Time for his next lesson. Jackson met his friend Beth in the second half of 2012 through a mutual friend. They shared some of their past experiences as friends do. They got along quite well. One morning

Jackson received a phone call from Beth; her and Annie had been in touch as Beth was looking to buy some jewellery that Annie sold online. This initial communication escalated into over two hours of phone banter very late one night. Beth informed Jackson she felt pulled into the conversation, he was the topic of the night. They bantered, pushed and prodded each other. Some of the conversation was conveyed to him. After all he'd been through and the sharing with Beth, Jackson was rocked by this whole turn of events. He told Beth that she had stirred a hornets' nest. He wasn't sure what was going come to from all this but he had a very bad feeling. Jackson and Beth's friendship ended there.

Two days later, Jackson's phone rang in the early morning. He answered it only to hear Annie's voice (he hadn't spoken to her for months). She dramatically asked, "Is it true?" He had no idea what she was talking about and hung up. Annie called again and mentioned something about paedophilia. He hung up again. Annie then sent a photo to his phone of a web page written about him. Naturally this caught Jackson's attention. It was supposedly written by an anonymous mother that was currently dating him, speaking out that the world must know that he was a paedophile. The site mentioned that she was in a relationship with him, where he lived, a brief description of him, Jacksons full name and that he had violated her daughter. Jackson had been enjoying living alone since Annie. He was absolutely shell shocked someone could write such a thing. How could anyone be so cruel?

Annie persisted in calling so Jackson decided he'd hear what was going on. When he answered she quickly fired questions at him, most of them centered on the relationship between he and Beth. He realised then that this was her real focus and concern. Jackson said, "It's all bullshit" and hung up. He received many texts from Annie over the next few days. That morning Jackson went to the local police station and asked what he could do about the web page. The officer informed him that *it cannot be traced, that this sort of thing happens all the time. He then looked at the picture sent from Annie and noted the total views for the site. There were only five. The officer said it's probable that the person whom created the site is likely to be the one going into the site to assess it upon completion. He offered to Jackson; "It's not is as if you're under investigation. "Jackson responded, "I wish I was so that the lying person who wrote this could be found."*

It's pretty safe to say Annie and Jackson's ex-wife were not friends. But once again, it was evident through text messages he'd received that they were in contact again within a day or so of the web page fiasco. A couple of weeks after Annie rang him, his ex-wife's lawyers sent a letter expressing their concern about the web page and wanted an explanation for it. A number of times Jackson Googled his name to see if he could find the site. He was unsuccessful, even two weeks after the photo had been sent to him. A copy of the site and his ex-wife's first page on Google was forwarded to him as evidence for the site in court. Jackson found it interesting that it was on her first Google page at the top which showed regularity. Part of his response was, "It appears she knows more about this site and the circumstances surrounding it than I do." This of course he could not prove.

It's amazing what can bring people together. Sometimes it may just be the pain and suffering that they share even though their stories or ideas at times oppose each other. Unfortunately, projecting or transferring this pain will only at best (for lack of a better word) give you a short illusionary and temporary *fix*. A distraction from what is actually going on.

There were great lessons in the above-mentioned experience.

I would like you to consider these following questions;

- If you were in Jackson's shoes, how long do you feel it would take you to accept and process being slandered like this over the internet?

- What lessons would you have learned?

Take time to reflect and feel your answers.

Jackson did fulfil his requirements to be assessed and reports were written for the court by the respective psychologists, giving him a clean bill of mental health. This of course was contested by his ex-wife, therefore requiring them to be cross examined by her on the stand. Their findings and in-depth reports were not enough. The judge felt she had the right to prove them wrong and question their very qualifications and experience in such matters. Bearing in mind she has no qualifications in mental health! This further delayed unsupervised access to Jackson's children for months.

I've had some similar experiences to Jackson's. Many of us have to varying degrees.

In my situation, it took me two days to process, accept and understand an internet experience that to some degree, reflected in Jackson's story. To allow myself to feel free again. How, you may ask? Let me tell you the most amazing experience that changed my life forever.

CHAPTER 5

REFLECTING - THE KEY TO CHANGE

THESE NEXT EXPERIENCES changed my life, I have never been the same since.

I felt angry at not being able to speak with my son in July 2012. I was able to feel it. I was hurting inside, It was a natural response. I then realised how much his mother in the phone call was hurting, even if she blamed me, I could not hold that against her. I refuse to gage how much I open my heart based on another's view of me or my circumstances. It makes no sense. A number of questions came to me whilst driving to an appointment which led to an amazing new outlook on life itself!

The first question that arose; "What am I really seeking from this person that's causing me pain?" My heart then answered back, "Why can't she see me? Why can't she see my heart?" The answer to this was that it was impossible, we did not even speak. On top of this I knew she was hurting too much to see me. Upon realising this I was able to let it go. It was not necessary anymore, the idea of needing her approval simply melted away.

That led to the next question which mysteriously popped into my mind's eye... the *big one*. I enquired within me, "After all the pain and hurt projected onto me, and all the lies, conflict and misunderstandings that have been said, if the circumstances were completely reversed and my kids were with me, would I at the very least stop or distract my kids from speaking with their mother on the phone?" I received my answer instantly, "I could not." It wasn't in me. I knew it would eat into my conscience like cancer. I then asked myself what I would have to be feeling to not be aware of that guilt. I realised that I would have to be fully immersed in *my own thoughts, my own suffering, my own pain*. In that moment I knew that it wasn't personal. It was a way of coping for her. As I would have had to be immersed in *my thoughts and feelings* of pain and suffering, so was she. At that moment I realised for the first time in my entire life I had a beautiful heart. I truly felt it.

During this reflecting I was driving to Busselton for a meeting. Questioning my feelings, while being open to understanding myself and others, allowed me to break down barriers that were stopping me from accessing my heart. This created an unforeseen domino effect to other false ideas I had clung to. In that moment, when I realised I wasn't causing the suffering within my ex-wife, I felt my true heart.

Feelings of intense love poured through me. I felt I was going to explode. As this began, I saw my mind reaching out trying to create a scenario to cover what I had dis-covered, trying to hook or capture me. It went as quick as it came as I fell into laughter, laughing out loud. I knew in that moment that no thought can ever taint or cover what I had found. I felt overwhelmed with love as I drove, I wanted to stop and hug every tree. I would've if I wasn't running late at the time, not that I was feeling at all concerned. Everything was just perfect.

The more love I felt, the more I gave back to nature all around me. At the same time, I knew that what I had finally found, is in everyone... universal heart. It is our natural way! Everyone shows softness, love and nurturing at times but mostly with close family or with people they feel they can trust. We all have the capacity, it is only fear, pain and anger that blinds us through misunderstanding. That pure love is in us all, at all times!

Imagine if you could live in an absolutely perfect loving home, with everything you could ever need, lacking nothing at all. In this *profound beauty of your heart,* you are complete. Now imagine if you only lived in your home when you felt loved by another. Each time you do not feel that love from your partner or anyone else on the planet, you lock yourself out. This includes any fears that may be sparked by some random person or even social media, you'd rarely return to your heart, if at all.

Unfortunately, that is what almost all of us do. Don't you deserve more? Don't we all? That home is your heart just waiting to be occupied. People spend countless dollars building a false home. Your perfect home in your heart is completely free from more than you could imagine. It won't allow you to bring your baggage inside, because it is absolutely not needed.

When you can accept *your many ways or character* irrespective of another's view, then you can finally understand and accept another's. There is a little potential trap here though, this does not necessarily mean you agree with their view. You may understand where another is coming from, irrespective of their choices. You can be free from trying to control your whole environment and those around you. Wouldn't you like to be free from trying to hold everything together? This is absolutely not necessary and actually impossible, but it is what so many people do. Being caught in this illusion restricts your flow on many levels and you carry that tension around with you wherever you are. This, over a period may lead to ill health or *dis-ease*.

To find acceptance within doesn't mean everything will always be *light and fluffy*. Or that you will accept unacceptable behaviour. You just stop buying into another person's false *story*. This means you stop supporting and intensifying another's self-defeating, self-inflicting and emotional turmoil. True support is to understand, empathise and encourage another to work through one's own entrapments, but only when *they are ready*, not when *you are ready*.

It is a fact that if someone is trying to be superior, it is purely because they feel inferior within. Otherwise no game or position would be played at all, no pushing or pulling. We would just communicate healthily, sharing, listening and understanding.

My understandings were crucial in dealing with the internet story, touched on at the end of chapter 4. There was actually nothing I could do about it. I couldn't imagine making up something like that out of my own pain. It clearly shows the place those people or that person must have been in. I could have wished more pain upon them, like many possibly would have, but how could that help anyone? As far as I could see, they were already suffering far more than I.

Let those that are able to see me, see me. Not everyone will be able to do so. It would be foolish of me to expect everyone to relate to me or even want to. We are all on different paths. Not everyone's will resonate with mine.

In another valuable lesson I've learned, when I hear negative views of someone I may be cautious from their view or opinion, but I will still rely upon my own intuition or feeling from relating with that person referenced. I feel it is healthy to be cautious in general and not project or rush to form an opinion. That is, as we all know, *respect must be earned*. I would much rather have a few friends that I resonate with, whom I trust, than reactionary friends in which I have to modify myself for their approval, fearing their disapproval. When you finally approve of yourself on a very deep level, those friends tend to fall away.

When you look closely, many experiences will reveal aspects of yourself. What you are holding onto and what you need to let go of. Letting go by ignoring is a long way from letting go through understanding. They are opposite in fact. The latter is the ultimate goal as you cannot let go until you truly do understand. Look closely, the understanding you need is far closer than you can possibly imagine and it's the greatest goal or outcome.

In April 2013, believing Jackson had satisfied his court orders with positive reports from the child supervisors and the clinical psychologist. The magistrate informed him that all he needed was to see a psychiatrist for five visits, the rest had been satisfied. He mentioned it wasn't clearly written in the orders. The magistrate agreed but said it was for Jackson's protection as much as his kids. He had handled his case since the start and there had been continuous flak toward him over the years. Jackson could not dispute his reasoning.

The final psych appointments started with psychiatrist Wilson; final assessor as agreed in court. Lucky for Jackson, life had saved the best for last. In fairness, psychologist Jones was under the influence of Annie but why he would prescribe medication without speaking to Jackson on his own and submit letters from Annie after their separation, was reckless and unprofessional. Psychologist Davis (as ordered and agreed 25 sessions) was able to get a more rounded picture and Jackson felt rapport with him from the start. Psychologist Smith seemed to be fixated on his views from the beginning and bragged to Jackson that he had acquired every qualification a psychologist could get, attempting to enforce an authoritarian view. Nothing Jackson could have said would have swayed that. Psychiatrist Wilson came across as very sharp, witty and understanding. Jackson was surprised after feeling judged or misunderstood by psychologist Jones and Smith how open he could be with Wilson. It was a breath of fresh air.

This story isn't the most important part of this book, it's the lessons gained along the way. I've tried to keep this chapter as short as possible. One can get lost in the detail. I don't wish that for you. The more you resonate with these experiences, the more I hope you will gain courage to work through your own challenges. No matter what happens in our lives, there is always hope.

CHAPTER 6

FINDING WORTH - BE TRUE TO YOU

KNOW IT.

FEEL IT.

LIVE IT.

OUR THINKING CAN be a blessing in disguise. Our true test to what we think we know and what we truly know, is in our freedom from our thoughts or our lack of attachment to our thoughts. When you have a true awakening moment, you will find no thoughts are able to capture you. They appear almost laughable. There is no interest in where they lead because deep within you, you know that all thoughts are void of any substance at all. This becomes clearer as you begin to feel your heart like never before.

We have all been challenged by others trying to firmly assert their view over ours. Other people personally challenging what I say, think and feel was my greatest lesson. I had to learn to trust my heart, my intuition, my way. Against the grain of others at times and even to this day. Many entertain their fears on why not to do things. To find our way we must trust our intuition, it recalibrates our inner compass, revealing our path. That is enough, the joy and excitement of the journey is in the potential of every step. Trying to unravel the future before each step will only serve to limit our view, our experience. Trust your gut against all odds and be open to possibilities.

Up until early 2012 Jackson's experience when confronted by strong idealistic women was to shut down mentally and emotionally during certain traumatic moments without being able to access any cognitive thinking. His mind would feel foggy and inaccessible. It's how Jackson learned to cope from a very young age. He just couldn't find the words. Jackson therefore went along with women on many occasions through fear of more conflict.

There are several reasons in my experience why another may desperately try to convince you to believe their view or ideas. They may feel your current path doesn't serve you or is destructive, therefore try to change your course for your own physical protection.

If someone is persistent in delivering or superimposing their view over yours, displaying strong signs of annoyance or anger, *they* are vulnerable/insecure, irrespective of how they try to justify or convince you that it is for *your benefit*. Often, they themselves fully believe this. They are protecting an idea, which is extremely vulnerable.

Truth of heart and mind which is essentially one, needs no protection, for it cannot be defiled, tainted or destroyed. It can only be discovered. It's mere essence when truly felt, cuts through all illusion.

Since experiencing my heart for the first time, my life experiences have dramatically changed. Mostly people are very open toward me, although my resolve is still tested at times. When I truly want to be heard, I connect or express by waiting for my heartfelt understanding and speak from there. What once I may have considered weak, disempowering or soft is now far more potent. It may be as simple as asking, *please do the right thing*. Words alone are not powerful. It is where they come from that matters. That *energy* is carried and only heart can permeate all barriers irrespective of outside appearances.

Softness is the way through, for understanding. Rarely can you change what another feels. The firmer you are the more steadfast they become. Confidence (not stubbornness) immersed in heart through softness will slowly but effectively permeate their exterior. Sometimes only after they have walked away, but the more from the heart you are the sooner they will feel you. Even if you are lost in the moment and feel anger or frustration, your final word or message must be immersed in softness.

You have nothing to prove. This will release yourself of any guilt or burden. When we are calm and clear we wish pain and suffering on no one. Unfortunately, when another is in a lot of pain it may take years for the softness to get through. Just remember, the softer and more genuine you are, the sooner they will see or feel the turmoil around both of your experiences. To be completely genuine there has to be no attachment to the outcome. Your friend or partner on some level will know and feel the difference, even without being consciously aware of it. To offer this, is to offer them a sense of self-empowerment which supports true change, allowing them to grow and potentially trust themselves on their journey and yours.

A firm approach from others may reveal how they are feeling - unnurtured, unheard, unappreciated and misunderstood. Even if this does not appear necessarily true, it is how they are feeling. Many people do not feel worthy therefore have not yet fully discovered the benefits of their own pure, soft, loving and nurturing heart. That is why they are reaching out. They are in pain. It is not a reflection of you, it is a reflection of their self that they are caught in. So, try to understand and do your best not to take it personally.

Even if they love you, you may be on some level filling a void within them (or so they would like) at this time. They may even subconsciously try to keep you and others around for their 'safety and comfort'. Although it may trap them into a self-defeating pattern that causes suffering, a sense of comfort may be felt purely because 'it is what they know' (familiarity and conditioning). Ultimately all self-defeating projections or patterns must be unraveled.

CHAPTER 7

EBB AND FLOW - LETTING GO

IT IS THE to-ing and fro-ing that ultimately leads us back home to our true nature. That back and forth movement ensures we move forward and constantly tests our resolve. Obviously if you keep getting hooked, you have not yet been able to see though those thoughts. Nothing you become hooked on will be seen through and I mean *nothing*, if you do not turn that piercing light of discrimination into yourself.

You must see what you crave from another. You must be completely honest (which may not be easy). We crave from another what we think we lack inside. An absolute truth is that we lack nothing. That is the truth at all times. It is only the belief within our thoughts that is stopping us from going beyond that veil. If you excuse bad behaviour, what we are effectively saying is, "It is someone else's fault I am like this" or "My behaviour is acceptable because of how you are." This belief will stop you from looking at yourself with any essential depth, therefore you will remain caught. You are believing you have no power over your life, no self-control. This is completely false.

No matter how much you may want to set yourself free from this illusionary realm, it is impossible so long as you hang on to even one idea or thought. You are solely responsible for you. Knowing this, you may start understanding the personal entrapments of your mind. Even seeing through one thought will start setting yourself free from the limiting confines of our thinking. The more shackles you break, the more you will start enjoying and embracing life's journey.

True living can only ever be about the journey, for the destination can never be truly known until you *arrive*. Therefore, any idea that you may have for the destination of what it looks like, tastes like or feels like, can at best be only a guess. An interpretation of what you may have heard or read can only ever be that. Belief in this interpretation may plant false ideas or may serve only as a barrier or restriction. There are many ways to describe true heart and if we all had to choose a word that best describes it, we would come up with many varied answers. Even the same answers would be unique in the experience of heart. We are one, the same source encompasses us all, but we are beautifully unique.

To find our true destination we must look inwards, not outwards. Most just haven't realized it, yet. Our true essence is in us, around us and is all that is, at all times. Without it we could not exist. Only doubt, anger, fear or pain may give the feeling of that *lost connection,* but this is *literally impossible.*

In many cases, it does not take much investigating to see through our thinking. It's just a matter of training ourselves to know how. As the Great Hans Raj Maharai from Sacha Dham Ashram in India used to say, "Slowly, slowly." Having an expectation or an idea of how quickly you should progress is of course another entrapment of our thinking and will also have to be seen through. I'd suggest starting with the easiest, less challenging thoughts to see through and progress from there. It's the ones you are *least attached to*, which on one level means, *the thoughts you are gaining the least from.*

CHAPTER 8

EMBRACING CHANGE - BREAKING THE MOULD

IT'S AMAZING ON the outset looking in on the three to four years of Jackson's life from 2009. He kept himself fully preoccupied. He was lonely and miserable most of the time. Jackson only had energy for work, a little sport and some running around for his kids. He didn't feel fully present with them. Jackson didn't feel fully present at all. He was around 37 and he remembered pushing himself to be able to physically do what he used to. He was trying for that sense of freedom or joy he used to get from sport, it was always his escape.

The more Jackson pushed, the worse he became. His energy continued to suffer and diminish over the next few years. He drove himself into the ground. Jackson starting to write extracts for a book just before everything transpired. What he wrote was technically correct but little was he to know he was about to be tested on all of it. This was the beginning of the end of his life as he knew it. The toughest and in the end, the most liberating three years of Jackson's life.

It's the soil soaked in the right amount of shit that allows plants to flourish most and the universe ensures that every soil has the right amount for each and every one of us. It's the willingness to open without fear that's the key. Like a beautiful flower radiating all its beauty. What else to do? Procrastinate about the soil or weather? What a waste.

The key to empowering ourselves and others is not by putting them in a box. It is by setting them free and showing them their uniqueness. The risk of categorising people is, it may lead us to accept that *this is just the way we are*. Personality traits show patterns, but it is not who we are. It is merely a stepping stone. It's important to discover ourselves and understand certain experiences, but ultimately, we are not victims of circumstances. These experiences show us aspects of ourselves, which if you look hard enough, will lead you home to your heart.

We are unique, but there are no excuses for accepting an idea or concept that serves only to lock us into a disempowered space. Understanding your personality traits may give you a healthier perspective or a way to cope. But how do you pull yourself out of negative habits? How do we begin to see?

A good start is by telling yourself you deserve more. Looking for more, finding a spark, something that gives you a sense of hope or happiness. It is the single most important journey of your entire life, the search for true happiness, joy and love is all within you and for you alone to discover and only *you* can walk your path. That's a beautiful thing!

To decipher your own personal map to your heart you only need to start trusting your heart or intuition (this is maturing). Not your thoughts, fears or anyone else's (this will entrap you ever more deeply in misery and suffering). It would be like following someone lost that has never been home and has no understanding of directions, they can only see from their limited experiences, fearing certain spaces or places, having not done *the internal work*, causes more confusion (this is what happened to Jackson).

We will all be challenged by another's experiences, views, thoughts and feelings. This tests our resolve, our choices. Jackson certainly was! But only your very own truth or intuition will guide you all the way home. The more you invest in it, the more it will reveal. It will show you more beauty than you could possibly imagine within you.

Many have made the journey but no one else knows your path. Sure others may inspire or guide you, but every step is your own. You are ultimately in control of your own destiny. A great mistake many make is in the false idea; if it feels real, it must be real.

The only true denominator is love and integrity. This is something we all embody. Our only block is the belief in our limited thoughts and ideas of pain, fear and suffering which leads to anger. Even through all this pain the truth always remains within us all. How often, after a realisation when reflecting on a past situation, do we realise that we actually knew what the right thing to do was all along, we just couldn't see it at the time? We only lack the belief in our self.

Looking at my own past, asking myself questions and answering truthfully as best I could really enabled me to begin disentangling myself from the many traps of my thinking. Ultimately this process is what set me free from the negative entrapments of my thoughts. When I tasted my heart for the first time, I realised that no thought could ever alter the truth of my heart. I discovered something very beautiful. It is only the belief in our thoughts that bind us. Therefore, it can only ever be our own personal journey within. We cannot blame another for our thinking. It makes no sense.

Less aware minds living on auto pilot (without awareness) may have the job, the house and the car but have restricted that depth of joy available within. There's nothing wrong with having all these things and outward success. The only true difference is self-awareness which makes all the difference in the world. Obviously, children are conditioned without fully being aware of it, or how much it will affect their life. While this is taking place children still get lost in the *moment (present)*, therefore still experiencing joy on a deeper level than many adults. Generally, children tend to be less encased in ideas or fear. True joy is only truly experienced in the present or 'now' moment. On autopilot, after a while the vast majority of us *ultimately* will feel something is missing and will be forced to face our hidden *conditioned cycles or patterns*, which creates turmoil for ourselves and those around us.

Our thoughts, even from universal mind or consciousness are ours and ours alone as long as we are personally attached to them.

It's best to watch them and enjoy the show, don't take them so seriously and learn to laugh. In saying that, as long as you are caught or distracted by your negative thinking, don't pass it off as nothing. There is something for you to do, to see through or understand. Life will always affect your emotions to a degree, but until you stop losing yourself in the emotion, not questioning it or reliving it over and over, possibly blaming another, you are still trapped by a false idea. This idea would have you believe you are a victim and that you are powerless to change anything.

It's true, people may reflect our thoughts of ourselves. Although being interdependent we are individually in control of our life or happiness, but unfortunately our thoughts are mostly out of control. We need to realise this before we can truly start maturing and breaking through our false ideas. Only then can we set ourselves free.

CHAPTER 9

SELF WORTH - WHERE TO DRAW THE LINE

I USED TO SEEK approval for most of my life, trying to find value by being valued by another, moulding myself. Even looking for validation from women that I was a man. What a way to live. Everyone's values, experiences and ideas of what being whole or complete is, differs immensely. If you look closely, almost everyone is living in a way that promotes unhappiness or misery. We have all heard the term, *'We reap what we sow'*. Many of us know this intellectually but are so caught on autopilot, through fear, we don't know how to pull ourselves out, or change a situation to benefit us, or encourage self-awareness. Only through self-awareness can we disengage from our own personal self-defeating *autopilot* within us.

We may not change another's opinion. Only when one is open to possibility can we spark something within. It is even more likely if they are already open and self-reflective (only through self-reflection can one break through this illusionary realm in which we are caught). This is the fastest way to discover the true depths of your heart. So many great beings have asked themselves a question through reflection. The divine timing is perfect (as always) and they have worked through and surrendered enough for that final question to shatter the remaining ideas or thoughts that were mistaken to be real. It has always been said that it is only the belief in our thoughts that stop us from discovering our true self.

It's important to note when looking into the pain and entrapments of your thoughts when caught in suffering, if someone tries to *gain* from *playing the victim* or blaming, it sets them up to feel on some level that they can gain from another. This is a very vulnerable place for a number of reasons.

Most importantly it discourages them from finding and trusting their own heart, therefore they invest in manipulation rather than truth by protecting a *story* for a *false* sense of power. Whatever they may think they are gaining is superficial and will not last. This often locks them into a self-defeating cycle where ultimately, they expand their story to justify their pain, which is enhanced from the feeling of being a long way from their heart. People like this are often aggressive, fragile, reactive and full of pain (this pain is a misunderstanding from their own thinking). It takes ultimate courage to face your own thoughts and it is most often the last place we examine. This is why we suffer for so long. Often these people intensely control their environment for a fleeting sense of peace. As long as your happiness is dependent on your surroundings, on some level you are believing you are a victim of your circumstances. This could not be further from the truth!

If I was to try to gain approval from any being who is seeking peace or fulfilment outside of themselves, I would be sending them a message that it is okay to continue this pattern. I would be therefore giving my power away to someone that doesn't even understand their own. It would be like giving a weapon to a child. Anyone who *takes power* has not realised their heart, therefore, cannot fully support you or themselves. These people may encourage you up to a point, but will do their best to ensure you don't leave their *shadow*. I would much rather not encourage self-defeating behaviour. There are a number of ways we may try to gain from another. The sooner we realise this ultimately cannot fulfil us, the sooner we will start looking within and start breaking through our self-defeating thoughts and ideas.

Ego can be very elusive and subtle. If I was to try to protect another in a restricting or domineering manner from anything that *I feel* is not serving them, based on my mind made insights or understandings, then *I* would be playing God. That would be ego.

Life gives everyone exactly what they need to grow, this does include support around them and the possible challenges this may also bring. Who are we to say we know better? To inject oneself into one's life without consent or a mutual understanding would be ego.

Life isn't held together by me or my ideas. What a relief that is. All I need to do is to be true to myself and cultivate my heart. The rest is taken care of. I could not truly know all the reasons why something happens, even though I cannot see something, this does not mean it is not possible. We used to think the world was flat and flying was impossible. Be open to any and all possibilities. There is karma and so many things at play and miracles happen every day.

If I want to improve a relationship with anyone, there are ways. But the goals are to heal yourself within any given situation, not change anyone else. It just so happens that the love, healing and understanding you gain (even on subtle levels) ripples out affecting others.

There are meditative techniques which can work wonders and help release suffering. There will be a meditation at the end of this book. The techniques are not mine. The meditation has had amazing results with myself and my friends. But the focus is on healing yourself and your situation. When this occurs, the situation truly changes. It backs up the old saying "If you want to heal the world, start with yourself."

CHAPTER 10

FOCUS ON YOU - BECOME YOUR OWN PRIORITY

HAVE NO EXPECTATION of another and be true to yourself, this enables self-nurturing and you will be at your happiest. *This does not mean you won't be challenged*! Just remember, your amazing life's journey inward is dependent on no one. Don't preoccupy yourself on what another should learn, only on what *you* need to release and learn. When you truly change, everything changes. When you truly change you lose the attachment to change (but you may still *encourage* it in others). Until this happens you cannot remain in the present. We often tell ourselves that things around us must change before we can find joy. This is a false idea.

You cannot be true to yourself while there is hate and fear in your heart. You can follow your intuition as best you can, rationalise and calculate your way through, but until you become intimate with your heart, feeling its purity *and in that knowing, recognise that all hearts are pure*, you are more prone to be swayed based on your pain, fears and emotions.

When you truly see yourself (heart) no one else needs to see you. That neediness dissipates and you are left with an open, pure undefiled love that doesn't rely on any circumstances for it to shine. This allows for true compassion, seeing through relative perceived flaws, even though you may not accept another's behaviour. So instead of wishing for them to share your or another's pain, it's replaced with a yearning for them to grow, awaken or discover that purity within, like a parent supporting a child.

We can only truly appreciate in others what we truly see or recognise in ourselves. What does this mean?

There are certain qualities that you will feel, have an understanding of and appreciate. This promotes love and acceptance as you realise that you are not lacking in these areas, therefore we can encourage another to discover this for themselves within.

Other qualities you will feel, but you may lack the insight or understanding to appreciate. Usually an unresolved emotion or emotions are attached to certain traits invoking reactions which may border on pain, anger or jealousy. These emotions stem from fear.

Then there are other traits we are so afraid of that we fear it in almost everyone. We judge others harshly for this, but often refuse to see these qualities in ourselves even though it may be at the forefront of our personality.

In reality the emotional make up in our psyche is *basically* the same although our experience differs with everyone which in turn may vastly affect the way in which we receive information and our environment. But the fact that we share so much should help us to be more understanding of ourselves and others. Enabling us to be far less critical and more nurturing and supportive to everyone including our self.

There is a vast difference between intelligence and wisdom! It has been said many times over, 'if you can know yourself then you can know another'. This is profoundly true. When you can taste or sense your own heart you can walk open hearted without the need of an idea of yourself or another, rather you meet them from a balanced, neutral and grounded state of openness. You trust your heart, knowing and intuition to handle what unfolds in front of you. You can be completely void of ideas or scenarios predicting how things should unfold or how you should protect yourself or cope in certain circumstances. You may proceed with caution rather than a projection or fear. This is an example of true *surrender* which is the key to freedom by *trusting yourself and letting go!*

CHAPTER 11

STOP THE DELUSION - TRICKS OF THE MIND

ONE CAN NEVER truly see until they let go of what they think true seeing is.

One can never arrive until they let go of what the destination looks like.

One can never truly feel until they drop their idea of what they should and shouldn't feel.

All false ideas point to something being misunderstood within you! Forget blaming others, this is nothing more than a distraction. A trick of your mind to stop you going deeper. Why? There are countless reasons but they all lead back to the same source. Doubting your heart and self-worth, therefore minimising your capacity for understanding. This shows unresolved fear and pain within. Letting or allowing your walls to come down integrates understanding, offering a new found freedom and deeper access to yourself and others. Each time this happens it causes a change within your realm of experience which on some level is an awakening. You gain more access to the *real* you. This in turn creates change around you as well. Even if the same apparent tests or similar circumstances return, you will view it in a new light, *it's a new opportunity*. A mistake many make is, when a familiar challenge confronts us once again, we assume that we have failed. This is not true. It's just another opportunity for deeper understanding.

All experiences give you an opportunity to grow, digest information, discover and express. We must learn to enjoy the process and remember where it leads. It is of utmost importance to accept what you cannot change, for it's happening whether you accept it or not. To surrender to this truth will actually give you a real sense of freedom. To deny yourself this reality will keep you bound to pain, anger and frustration. Accepting this will help through the more intense and painful lessons in life. The ones that give you the greatest opportunity for growth.

Embrace your personality but go beyond it! Based on our experiences we all have differing character traits. There are no excuses to behaving indiscriminately. Stopping your search at certain *stereotypes* which we all have, is nowhere near deep enough. These stereotypes may give a certain explanation of some behaviours but this is far from who we are. It may even momentarily quench your thirst, but it is like discovering a lake when there is a whole ocean out there. An ocean that knows no bounds and has limitless depths. As entertaining as putting things in an acceptable box for you is (and what a relief you may feel), it will only ever be temporary.

Learn to love and accept your personality. The more you can accept yours, the more you can accept and understand another's. As you grow to understand your wants and needs and differentiate between the two, the easier things will become.

It's my experience that life will give you what you need, not necessarily what *you* think you need, unless there is a lesson in it for you. All things good or bad may reveal aspects of yourself to take you deeper, work through, or loosen your grip from. There is nothing we need to hold together in our surroundings. This is only ever an illusion. Most get caught on this for many reasons and are afraid to let go, or even risk seeing if it is true. A sign of trying to do the impossible and hold things together around you; when you are thinking or talking about it, your breath becomes short or shallow. On some level you are trying to control or restrict your environment for your happiness, even though you may tell yourself it is for the happiness or benefit of another. If you tune into this *energetic* flow you will realise you are actually restricting the flow of your heart and the people around you as they modify/restrict *their way* in your presence. We have all felt these confines in the company of certain friends.

All that is required is to let go and trust your intuition, which will ultimately allow you access to your heart. Life supports you more at that point, than at any other time, as you will feel a more natural flow, you allow things to be as they are; whether you allow it or not, things are *as they are*. The point is; one way is liberating for you and one is not.

A trick of the mind is to say to yourself, "Okay, I will let go." Then what often happens is, we walk around trying to ignore our surroundings, pretending to be happy waiting for things to change, only to explode at some point in the near future when you see nothing has changed. *Fortunately*, we cannot fool our self or life. Pretending isn't changing. It is a misunderstanding to think everyone will conform to you or your environment when you truly change or let go. When your outlook changes for real, people *will* respond to you differently, but at that point it doesn't matter if things change, on a deep level you have realised that your happiness is dependent on no one. You see clearer, can express and clarify boundaries in a more nurturing and supportive way. You see through the emotional games and the pushing and pulling of those around you. It is recognised that it is never personal. It is due to their misunderstanding, their pain and their lack of knowing how to deal with it.

You will see through eyes of compassion, not pain. When you rest in your heart, your knowing, you give others the space to feel free to be themselves around you. When you rest in your heart, your natural capacity to nurture will dramatically increase without even seemingly doing anything different. Therefore, encouraging others to trust, open and be their self, they may not even consciously know why. They will naturally in most cases be uplifted around you which will automatically encourage better behaviour. What a great gift to offer those around you!

While we do not feel complete or whole, we will naturally swing from what one may call good or bad, positive or negative, up and down. This will continue until we discover the truth within our self, therefore within one and all. This on some level can be understood in the mind, but this can only be complete once the mind and heart are merged in understanding. What does this mean?

When something is truly understood, softness of heart, or compassion, is the predominant factor. It's natural and right to have reactions at certain times but when experiencing frustration or anger, it never lasts long, it is seen through. But if you cannot escape the entrapments of your thinking, it is clear that your mind understanding hasn't reached the heart yet. For only when the two are merged is there true deep understanding, softness, love and compassion.

Your story, that which possibly locks you into justifying the way you live and your pain or clarity is only ever about *your* understanding. It has *nothing* to do with anyone else's understanding or whether they *get it,* or even whether they understand or see you at all. This is actually irrelevant. When you truly see yourself (your heart) no one else needs to. If you are seeking another's approval you are missing your amazing heart and essence. You are caught in an *illusion*.

Reflecting and questioning your false ideas is the quickest way through, to be free from your own chains. Know that all your thoughts are false. Learn to let go. You don't have to know everything or believe what your mind tells you. It is all a trap, a test. Taking your *relative* ideas to be the absolute truth is your biggest cause of suffering. As long as you want another person to change or give you something for a sense of joy or peace, you will on some level *always* be suffering. There is nothing wrong with being given something, or even being spoiled. It's the attachment or dependency to these things that are the trap. It can quite easily leave you craving for more. No matter who it's from or how grand it may be, it can only at best give you a temporary false sense of worth or joy. No one can ever give you self-worth. It can only ever be discovered **within you, by you**!

We can only see what we are capable of seeing. We can only see clearly what we are not afraid of looking into. Looking into ourselves is deeply personal and has nothing to do with anyone. No one needs to even know what we discover. So it is obvious, if we are not capable at looking into our self, we are not capable of truly looking into another. This is why it is true that people often mirror ourselves, or we often see a reflection of ourselves in others. When you discover your heart, you will stop being fooled by your thoughts. You will understand another's pain because you understand your own. You will know that their reactions or ways are the result of their pain and lack of understanding within. It is not personal. It is because of *their* thinking, *not yours,* even if you are blamed, for this is impossible! You also know they have the potential to break through as you have. You stop condemning others even though you may choose to keep your distance. You will not be dependent on them being a certain way. You know that purity or essence within your heart is in all, everywhere. Therefore, you are free.

Keep it real. Most truths are not real at all, being based on one's own perspective (relative truths). From the outside looking in its easy to formulate a view or opinion to justify what we think or feel. Most befriend those whom support their *mistaken views* or are caught in the same trap. As our understanding or viewpoint changes so do our friends, or at least the way we communicate with each other does. Often if another's understanding or maturity falls too much out of sync with our own growth, the friendship falls away completely. It becomes obvious both needs are different and are not being met.

I have questions for you to consider:

1. Do you believe your viewpoint or understanding has always been the most correct?

2. Throughout your life, whilst conversing with a friend, have you mostly believed you were right and they were wrong?

3. How often have you been frustrated because you feel you have not been understood or taken seriously?

4. How often has your viewpoint changed over the years?

As you have matured and your understanding has grown, so has your views. Therefore, at what point have you spoken or known the absolute truth? These truths are only relative to a perspective. They are not real. I know they feel real but its only because we have vested interest in the outcome, whether it's for approval or self-gain. People on both sides of any situation have their own 'relative truths', their own perception. And both feel just as real and can be justified by each person involved.

Understanding this, you *can* actually support two friends with opposing views in a disagreement. You can remain neutral.

A grave misunderstanding is "if you understand where I'm coming from (my view) then you agree with me". This is not true. I often disagree with another's perspective but I can understand where they're coming from. I often offer this; "I can understand where you are coming from, many people would feel the same, it does hurt." But then I'd offer this in varied ways (depending on our connection), when the time feels right; "remaining in this space over time will not only maintain your pain but enhance it. There is another way to relieve your burden, to free yourself."

Knowing that our view or perspective constantly changes as we mature will allow us to see that it is a natural process. Therefore, there is no need to hold onto or justify it for years. What are you actually holding onto anyway, besides tension? No one owes you anything, only *you* owe it to yourself to let go! Otherwise it becomes your burden and yours alone. As these burdens compress over the years, you become more and more miserable, harder to be around.

The only way to continually suffer over the years is to remind yourself that you are suffering. I used to know that place. It's so exhausting! It wastes so much energy. The thing is, unless you remind people no one knows why you are suffering.

There *is* abuse on many levels and this is magnified when you are feeling broken within. There are times when you must escape a situation for your own safety and wellbeing. You need a safe space to heal. Excluding physical abuse, *ultimately*, it is never another's fault you are suffering, contrary to what you may think. It can only ever be yours, as previously mentioned, your thoughts are yours and yours alone, as long as you are identifying with them.

It is important not to be hard on yourself. Take time out, nurture and get in touch with what you feel. Allow yourself to *feel* often, make time, learn to understand yourself. It becomes very destructive to deny yourself time or to constantly distract yourself. Have the courage to discover what you are running from within.

Your feelings are important, they reveal much of what is going on. You can never run from them. It must be faced by each and every one of us. This is not optional. One *must* swim through the ocean of emotion. You do not need to worry. We all enter this world fully equipped to embark on this voyage. You just have to make a choice, for true joy and peace is across the other side.

CHAPTER 12

NEGATIVITY - BREAKING THE CYCLE

FEELING OR PLAYING 'the victim'. This can often come from feeling squashed or put down over a period of time as a child or even an adult. You feel like everything is against you. You have no luck. Looking at what others appear to have and comparing yourself or your situation, is a limiting and dangerous trap, distracting you from what is truly important.

Sometimes life will give you a run of bad luck. In my experience, when your direction needs to change, life whispers in your ear. If you don't listen it will give you a prod, then a push and ultimately your world will come crashing down around you if you don't heed the signs. As what happened to Jackson from 2009, he became lost, he fell into 'the victim'.

It's a very slippery slope once you start going into that victim space. There are a number of traps within this place.

Great beings have said 'Where your focus is, is what you are worshipping'. These words are so true.

These are the basic steps to falling into victimhood. Are you on this scale?:

- You begin focusing on your negative thoughts.

- You expect bad things to happen.

- You start reminding yourself of all the bad things that have happened.

- You start playing them over and over in your mind. Energy does follow thought and even on a physical level it becomes obvious how you are feeling. It affects your entire body.

- When we don't know how to deal with this negativity and our thoughts are out of control, we mirror our inner thinking externally and vent. This reinforces our new negative developing pattern.

- We find friends who are prepared to justify and support our story. This of course locks us in deeper.

- There is not much else you will talk about as the pain that comes with being a victim enhances. It is a feeling of being lost and worthless with no way out. In this space you will be lacking motivation and energy.

- You will seek out people who feel sorry for you. On an energy level, anyone who goes into your story and feels sorry for you, you will feed off. You will drain them and you will have a little more energy. We have all experienced both sides of this. This can continue for years.

From my experience anything that doesn't come from within you through understanding does not last. The problem is, when another whom is suffering or feeding your pain feeds that void, even if you feel a small temporary gain, it is enough to keep you locked into this pattern and feeding off others. The more someone supports your negativity, the more entrenched you become. This pattern is exhausting for all involved. It takes a massive amount of energy to maintain this thought pattern and in the end, it will wear you down and possibly break you.

It's not easy to break this habit but it can be done. Maybe after a while, even you will get sick of hearing your story and start to seek answers and clarity. It really comes down to breaking out of autopilot, that automatic negative cycle of the mind and becoming *aware*. This can be done by simply questioning your thoughts but you need to truly want to see what's going on.

Ultimately when you suffer long enough you will find a way to challenge your thoughts. This may take what feels like lifetimes, but *you do* have a choice. Just know that in this process, your thinking doesn't give in easily and will challenge you, but this is all part of the growth process and our quest for true understanding.

The bottom line is this: as real as this negative place feels, it is not real and never will be. You have fallen into a false idea of yourself. You are as you are; although you have certain character traits, you can never truly be defined. The eyes of the beholder are rarely clear enough. If you are blessed to meet a great saint or being, that live from heart (universal heart) that could truly see you and spoke of your potential, you could not understand or believe them in the victim space. Best to be open to your potential at all times, even if you're unsure of what that is.

The trap is our mind feeding our emotions, then our emotions feeding our mind and so on and so forth. In this cycle our reactions become more fragile. We have less control; we convince ourselves that if it feels real then it must be real. This is not true; it is very likely that while you are falling for and defending a painful emotional reaction, reliving it in your mind over and over, you are creating a neural pathway assigning *triggers*, which not only maintain, but magnifies future responses. In turn, burying you more deeply into suffering, limiting your life through fear of being *triggered further*.

What the mind does from believing a false idea and does extremely well, is to justify the idea. It will find anything to reinforce the negativity. Therefore, you will start seeing things from the glass is half empty perspective. You become very practiced at it. You can never discover your potential if you play the victim, at best you're just treading water. You have to want to break the minds cycle to begin to see through its illusionary story.

For over 20 years I had been wanting to see what is real and see through my mind's entrapments. I felt that my world (my ideas), had to be shattered as I was too encased. At times when I felt most broken, there is no way I could have conceded this view, I was just fighting to survive. As my yearning grew as I entered my late 30s, I was shown the quickest way home, into my heart. This Journey was over rougher terrain than I could ever have imagined, during a very short and intense few years of my life. The more lost I felt, the more I wanted answers. I'd been praying for the most direct route for years and I wanted it *now*! Be careful what you ask for. After the fire (challenges) ravages your life, everything is different. But you have to be prepared to walk through it and at times you won't believe you can. Often for me when I thought I'd worked through major challenges, the next wave would hit. But through vigilance and yearning for more understanding, breakthroughs came and walls crashed down, revealing new found freedoms.

Ultimately you will be forced to let go of all your ideas, for they are the ***only*** obstacles stopping you from discovering true joy and happiness within you. The crazy thing is all your ideas of yourself or another are completely false and can potentially change on a whim. How can that be real? And letting go of your thoughts does not mean you have none. You are just not attached to them because you know they are not real. It is said *"There is nothing wrong with having preferences, as long as you are not attached to them."* This is freedom!

When you make excuses for your negative thoughts you plan to fail and you invite more suffering into your life. Some of us become more and more miserable and have trouble coping, yet we do the same thing day after day. To create new feelings, we must be willing to create new experiences, or at the very least, be prepared to see something familiar in a whole new way. When we are suffering, it's the old way (old perceptions) that causes this suffering. Take a chance, try something different!

An out of control mind is not your friend. You cannot trust what it tells you, it will not help you or show you the way. It does not have the answers. In my experience, the reason we are suffering is purely because we are believing the mind chatter it offers. So why believe it at all? It will test you; it will trap you, anyway it can. Until you can truly see through it, it cannot be totally on your side.

Our mind is like a pack of wild horses, pulling our body along in a cart. At times they may be walking along relaxing, or on a rare occasion they may even stop for a rest. In that moment you may think, "I can control them, they do whatever I want." You may even coerce them to head a certain direction for a while, you may dangle a carrot or offer some type of reward for obedience. Then suddenly out of nowhere they get spooked, fear rushes in! They're off and racing again, out of control. No matter how much you shout or scream, they will not stop. Only when they are exhausted do they slow down or stop. You then blame whatever spooked them; the environment, a sound, another horse. You pretend due to the 'ruckus' it wasn't your fault.

Maybe you feel embarrassed or ashamed for the damage it's caused. It's far easier to blame your surroundings or the situation, but unfortunately, this will never actually give you control. The good news is there are reins attached to the horses. They can be tamed, but not through beating them up, trying to control them, babying or finding excuses for them. *Only through softness, understanding and nurturing can you ever access the reins.*

The mind cannot break through the mind, only your heart can. This is what surrendering actually means. Giving way for your heart. *This is true empowerment!*

You have to be open to possibilities. You have to reflect and ask what you are truly seeking or gaining from by falling into your minds-trap. You must get in touch with your gut feeling, your intuition and feel what resonates. If your answers don't ultimately point back to something about you, your needs (not anyone else's), then keep going, you haven't gone deep enough yet. This is the last place your mind wants to go. It can be painful but also liberating.

The key when reflecting is to do it with softness, not pain or judgements. You're not looking to judge merely seeking to know. The mind is like a hurt, lost child that cannot fully understand. You have to be soft and kind before he or she is open to receiving and gaining insight... and you can't teach a child overnight. It takes time and patience, so, do your best not to be hard on yourself. Allow as much time as you can, as often as you can, to nurture the *inner you*. Take a bath with candles and incense or take a nice relaxing stroll, take your time. Let your barriers down. It will enable your vision or insight to expand, discovering the real you.

I believe the tests of our mind is to drive us more deeply into ourselves, so in a sense, it's working for a higher purpose. But make no mistake, it will completely test our resolve. It will try every trick in the book to catch or ensnare us.

If you have a shred of doubt, your mind will find it. When you discover your heart, your purity, essence of being, your mind will finally stop fighting (you will have tamed the beast). You now know to the core that **nothing** the mind says, **no scenario** can affect or taint your purity within, from which you now live. You lose interest in where your thoughts are trying to lure you, your mind quietens. You are at peace!

CHAPTER 13

TRUST WHAT YOU KNOW AND FEEL, NOT YOUR DESIRE

WHAT I HAVE found in healthily dealing with projection from another's strong view point or verbal attack, is a little natural cycle; *Receive, Feel, Release.*

When something is said or done which creates pain within you, it is natural to feel any number of things, shock, pain, anger or disappointment. It's like someone throwing mud on your face. It can sting when it hits.

The mistake most people make is they think the mud belongs to them. It is a reflection of the doubt they feel within. They begin rubbing it all over their body. They are so distracted by it that they cannot distinguish the mud from themselves. They assume no one else can either. The mud sticks and sets on them and they can't stop talking about it, causing them more pain. They become the mud.

Some, during this process, will retaliate by picking up the first bit of mud they find and throwing it back. When it hits its mark, they are relieved because they feel that now the suffering is reciprocated (that will teach them). But this benefits no one.

What is the benefit to everyone walking around suffering and throwing mud?

It's hard to say how to respond or behave in all situations. That's not realistic. What is realistic is the place of integrity you can maintain or at least finish in, if you lose yourself in the moment.

You may at times have to be firm and cut ties. It's not about being submissive or weak, it's about learning to let go by coming to a place of peace and understanding within you, *before* you deliver your final message.

If you are accused of something you know you didn't do and they are not open to you, I'd say in most cases *stand strong* in your knowing, intuition or heart. Your heart, your honour, your integrity is worth expressing and standing up for.

The good news is, *you can* break the negative cycle in which most are caught and set yourself free from the turmoil from another's ideas or projections. Ceasing the *acting and reacting* without any real sense of control.

In my experience now, when the mud hits there is of course an initial reaction and I express depending on the pain, the accusation, or misunderstanding in the situation that I feel from them. I don't get all encased in their ideas and proceed to rub it all over me. Usually I make them aware of how they are addressing me and let them know how it makes me feel. It can be hard to *check in* with how you feel in the moment.

Other times, if they are completely closed or aggressive, I may *react* to create some space so I can leave or at least prohibit their invasion of my space. But as soon as you get the chance, stop and feel, the longer you take, the longer you are bound by the experience. I sit with it, feel it, try to get a sense of their pain and the momentum behind it. Not to minimise another's suffering, but this process gets easier and easier as you become clearer within. This is the pathway to true understanding, allowing yourself to process and let go.

Remember... this reflecting is for your understanding so you can let go. It is not for them. If you are being attacked through anger, they are not looking to you for help or understanding (this cannot take place until they are calm and open). They are looking to blame and you're it, guilty or not. It is worth remembering, the more pain one feels the less one sees. There is one exception to this. It happens to all of us at some point and it really assisted me in breaking down barriers when I have been lost and angry. On rare occasions when one is suffering, in pain and feeling vulnerable, or feels there is no way out, one can surrender and walls will come crashing down. This can potentially become an *'enlightening'* experience.

I have found there are two key points that need to be grasped in not buying into another's turmoil to facilitate letting go.

This first point is that we can rarely prove an aggressor wrong even if they are wrong. If they were open to receive you, their whole approach would be different. Trying to convince them your view may be seeking their approval. This competition can potentially feed them and create turmoil for the both of you, ultimately draining everyone. They cannot have the upper hand here unless you give it to them. Alternately, with two strong personalities it can be like a tug of war, it wastes a lot of energy and no one wins.

Winning is never about hurting one more than the other. True victory is about understanding the pain and confusion within you, therefore releasing it. When journeying to the place of softness, resolution, peace and acceptance of who you are, it's best to always take the moral high ground. Be the first to rise above, try to not buy into the emotion and stop the dramatic cycle.

The second point is that you are not at the core of their pain. You may be a trigger for it either directly or indirectly. So now how do you respond to actually release the burden you're feeling? Responding through pain will not allow you to set yourself free. At the core of your heart you are a great lover, nurturer, extremely soft, compassionate and understanding. This is your natural way. Anything that doesn't align with this truth causes you to suffer.

You may feel a sense of release to retaliate, but it is a temporary fix and will often be followed by guilt. You are actually compounding your pain. It's best to understand the aggressor is suffering and that it is *not* personal in order to access this next step and release yourself from the hurt you may also feel. But until that understanding kicks in, knowing this process will curb the momentum and is worth practicing. I go to the softest part within me and feel. That place is not angry, or seeking vengeance. It is deeper, it feels the pain and sadness like an open wound. I'm okay to feel this, it won't break me. Although I don't bathe in it or rub it all over me, it merely gives me a clearer sense. It shows me what I need to let go of and heal. This is accessing your heart.

From here you need to express back to the person that which releases you, not them. This means your whole approach will be different. It will come from softness with no attachment, seeking no approval. This last statement can easily be misinterpreted. This soft place can also deliver a firm "No" or "It's over!" That place within knows what you need and how to deliver it. This will only deepen and become clearer the more you trust it and discover yourself. The distinguishing factor is, heart doesn't condemn. It's not who we think we are that really matters since we are the same underneath. It's the choices we make and how we choose to live that matters. As we align our self with the truth within us, everything else begins to fall into alignment, ultimately impacting our friends, family and environment.

CHAPTER 14

TRUE WISDOM OVER INTELLIGENCE

I BELIEVE ALL TRUE religions lead to God. Our concept of God is not important. It is the motivation or inspiration to live and express through the purity and kindness of heart that matters most, living the principals of truth and integrity.

Living happily has little to do with intelligence. There is even a risk of over analysing or theorising or further distraction. I would say an unchecked intelligent mind has more fuel to burn, potentially creating a bigger fire to see through. Don't get me wrong, there is nothing wrong with being smart. My point is the journey inward is available and accessible to everyone, regardless of intellect.

True wisdom to me is the other side of the coin to intelligence. That is, real deep inner knowing of heart and peace can be achieved by anyone, educated with distinctions or an illiterate being that's never been to school. As mentioned over and over, it purely comes down to intimately knowing yourself. No one can teach you that. People can inspire, send you love or heal you but *only you* can peel back your layers within. It's nice to resonate with someone or something that inspires you, offers you encouragement or a sense or confirmation on your path. I'm doing my best to do all of the above in an attempt to nurture you, open and understand you, just as you are trying to understand me. I aim to support and nurture you through my words.

I am here to tell you "It's okay," I know it hurts," I know you can make it," I have faith in you." We are not so different you and I, regardless of race, colour or culture. I believe there is a high probability you don't nurture yourself enough or barely at all, you are worth so much more. I'm passionate about my writing because I believe if I can discover my heart, *you can too*. I'm not a scientist, a doctor or a therapist. I've had my fair share of ups and downs and I'm still kicking, stronger and happier than ever. There are no excuses not to strive for happiness. You are so worth it!

I hope that I have, at the very least, in some way taken some pressure off. We all have incredible challenges at times. No one escapes karma and we all will answer for what we say and do. Whether you're in a relationship or not, those whom are just waiting for an opportunity to pounce or accuse you, are in pain and if you allow, they just may become one of your greatest teachers.

I'm not advising you to necessarily invite strangers into your life. You may look at what an*other is offering or has to say* on the periphery of your world. Use caution and trust your gut instincts. *Some people **are** best kept at a distance!*

Walk with courage, be true to you and set yourself free from your very own entrapments of your thoughts. It doesn't matter what another says or does, only you can steer your ship. It's more important now than ever. Take the wheel and set sail for your most important voyage yet. Set yourself free, only you hold the key!

CHAPTER 15

MEDITATION

MANY PEOPLE AVOID silence or meditation, having to keep busy all the time, or constantly distracting oneself with drinking, drugs, TV, video games or our phones. Most people are afraid to face their thoughts.

As previously mentioned, that mind chatter is nothing more than a false idea, an illusionary concept. When I ask people what percentage of their thoughts are real, they often come down to "Not many," So, then I ask "Tell me just one thought that is real." No one has been able to, because no one can!

Initially I'm not talking about the names of things, or the processes on how to solve or resolve things, although all existence is illusional (everything we perceive is pure energy, even that which appears solid is just varying densities of energy and contains infinite potential within).

This is a harder reality to grasp. This understanding though, even conceptually, may well assist, encourage or inspire a sense of relief for people looking to confront their fears or false ideas.

Meditation is great in so many ways. There are countless different practices. With this basic one below, you will at the very least gain insight into yourself. You will begin to become aware of your thoughts and their patterns. You may be amazed at the extraordinary things you believe and fall into while your thoughts go unchecked without awareness. If you haven't meditated before, you're not used to meditating or haven't done one in a while, I encourage you to take a few moments now to sit in silence. Try this simple but effective method (one I still use today, additionally at times focusing on listening or feeling nature all around me). Read the next few paragraphs before trying to meditate for a little more understanding.

Sit comfortably and close your eyes. Take a few deep breaths if you're unsettled in your mind, body or your breathing. Put your awareness on your breath, breathe through your nose if you can. If you have trouble then you can breathe through your mouth. Now allow yourself time to feel and relax. Keep focusing on your breath, slowly inhaling and exhaling.

It is likely you will be distracted by your thoughts (this happens to almost everyone). As soon as you become aware of this, bring your focus back to your breath. Each time you catch yourself following your thoughts, repeat this process. Even 5 minutes a day will help. Increase the meditation time when you feel comfortable, but if you don't feel you can at this point, don't beat yourself up over it. It's your journey, to be done in your time!

This meditation often reveals your vested interest in your thoughts. It may be work related or prioritising, it may be desire, fear or self-importance based. Going over the work schedule may be important, but it's not necessary all of the time, or it may also be fear related. Fear of failure, or of being judged. A simple remedy is to write down your thoughts and what you need to do for work and/or whatever else is at the forefront of your mind and let the rest go. When you start meditating, you begin to accelerate the process of freeing yourself. Subtly, it will bring awareness to the autopilot aspects of your mind and its entrapments. Slowly, slowly, be patient, it will get easier and over time you will become more aware and freer within.

Try a short meditation now…

How many thoughts did you get lost in? The good news is you can train your mind to catch and question your thoughts, therefore see through them. You can sow the soil and prepare for the most profound journey of your life.

I wish you all the greatest success in your life and your journey. May your presence serve to nourish and inspire your family and all those around you.

Live your life.
Love your life.
Enjoy your journey.

FOOD FOR THOUGHT

Further to the many contemplations and considerations within these chapters. I have written 'Food for Thought' as a summary, to ponder and set oneself free from the many confines of one's thoughts.

It is inspired by my witnessing of the profound experiences and openness of my friends and family. I feel we must correct our thinking to truly nurture ourselves, to be open to greater possibilities and a deeper, more meaningful life.

WHAT IS IN ME IS IN YOU

Immerse yourself in your beautiful profound softness. May it melt your walls so that you may see and feel the divine beauty within and around you.

What is in me IS in you! That profound beauty does not belong to me or come from me, but comes through me. As I surrender, my walls come down, allowing me to shine, encouraging others to do the same.

There is nothing to own or hold on to. It is the mere ownership and grasping that limits us. The eb and flow of life is natural. It pushes us forward, inward. Resisting this creates suffering, turmoil. Let go, embrace the flow, for greater things are ahead of you.

INNER CHILD

To nurture our inner child is to heal that pain within, of not being enough, unworthy, undervalued, misunderstood. As we are able to soften around infants, children and our pets, we must offer this softening to ourselves.

Our inner child is hurting, waiting for us. This is the hole we feel. We **MUST** nurture and console this aspect within for true, deep healing and understanding.

We must stop being harsh and angry toward ourselves. Our inner child will never heal, you will never feel whole. Softness is gentleness are the way.

Slowly, slowly when walls come down, we will cry, we will sob. As will a child when, after years of being ignored, in darkness, abandoned, judged, finally feels some rays of sunshine, a sense of warmth, of hope.

In time we must allow our inner child full access to ourselves through self-nurturing, gently comforting and showing willingness to support and overcome any and all obstacles. Cradle your heart like you would a child, focusing on love and tenderness.

Do not block negativity, but transform and transcend it from others by seeing it for what it is, an illusion. It is a test, an unrealized opinion, nothing more, by 'someone whom is hurting and cannot see'.

BE CAREFUL WITH WHOM YOU SEEK ADVICE

Look at whom you seek advice. If they are angry, they will show you and encourage anger. If they are harbouring pain, they will show you and encourage suffering. If they are jealous, they will encourage jealousy.

Seek understanding from someone peaceful, loving or nurturing. Someone whom truly offers this to themselves. Then you know it's real. They may be hard to find but they're out there and patiently waiting for you!

A true seer will support, encourage and inspire the innermost you, your inner child, your heart. They will see you even when you cannot see yourself. They will never judge you. They will encourage you to find 'your way' not theirs.

We are beautifully and perfectly unique. So, the pathway to our hearts, although similar to some, are our own.

Others whom are angry, confused, controlling or bitter on their own path, CANNOT know your path. Learn from others, but don't take on their ideas that they cannot actualise themselves. The evidence is in their demeanour, not their words.

Learn to trust your gut, your intuition. The more you do, the more supported your journey becomes.

Start questioning all those external and internal, self-defeating voices that are holding you back. The answers are within your heart, don't stop until you're free. Be prepared to peel back the layers. This may take some time, be patient and don't forget to nurture yourself along the way.

NEVER GIVE IN

The innermost you is profoundly beautiful; it is so worth the journey. You will not be disappointed. ALL the answers are within. If you still feel pain within, keep going, only true understanding will set you free.

The mind will keep coming up with 'answers', 'interpretations' or 'assessments' on where you are. Don't sell yourself short, never settle for an idea that restricts you. Be prepared to let all thoughts go, you will not lose yourself.

Letting go of our restrictive thoughts and ideas is how we actually find our self, our true self! Often whilst in solitude, we discover our deepest love and connection to everything.

Although the answers are within you, you don't have to take this journey alone. Connection encourages openness and openness brings in possibilities allowing for growth, awareness and expansion. Bringing in more love, happiness and fulfillment.

For more inspirations, go to ShaneSacha.com

Shane was born in the early 1970's in New South Wales, Australia. He likes a bit of mystery, so you'll have to figure out his age on your own.

He grew up kicking a ball around with his mates. He found he had a preference for the strangely shaped, oblong ones, so much so, he decided to do it professionally. Weird, I know but that's Shane pretty much all-round. Weird but in a nice way. Around the same time, he grew some muscles and thought he'd be a staunch bouncer for a few years. Ugg.

In the early 2000's he moved permanently to Western Australia and after much living and suffering he had a life-changing epiphany, taking his life on a completely different trajectory, filled with pure joy, self-love and discovery. Something achievable by all.

If Shane can do it, anyone can!
There IS hope for everyone ☺

www.ingramcontent.com/pod-product-compliance
Lightning Source LLC
LaVergne TN
LVHW091933070526
838200LV00068B/958